I0529469

ADVENTURE CARAVANNING WITH DOGS

IT NEVER RAINS BUT IT PAWS: A ROAD TRIP
THROUGH POLITICS AND A PANDEMIC

JACQUELINE LAMBERT

Copyright & Disclaimer

© 2022 Jacqueline M. Lambert

All rights reserved. This book or any portion thereof may not be reproduced or used in any manner whatsoever without the express written permission of the author except for the use of brief quotations in a book review.

First Paperback Edition 2022

Book Design and Formatting by Debbie Purse

The events and conversations in this book have been set down to the best of the author's ability, although some names and details may have been changed to protect the privacy of individuals.

All information, advice and tips in this book are based on the author's personal experience and do not constitute legal advice.

While every effort is made to ensure its veracity, there are no representations or warranties, express or implied, about the completeness, accuracy, reliability, suitability or availability with respect to the information, products or services contained in this book for any purpose. Any use of this information is at your own risk.

ISBN (paperback) 978-1-9993576-9-6

ISBN (ebook) 978-1-9993576-8-9

Contact:

Facebook: www.facebook.com/JacquelineLambertAuthor

Amazon: www.amazon.com/author/jacquelinelambert

Goodreads: https://www.goodreads.com/author/show/18672478.Jacqueline_Lambert

Blog: <u>www.WorldWideWalkies.com</u>

By the Same Author:

It's caravanning, but not as you know it...

Have you ever considered quitting work to travel?

When Jackie and hubby Mark were made redundant, they accidentally bought a caravan, then decided to sell up and tour full time with their four dogs. In their quest to Boldly Go Where No Van Has Gone Before, you will find Caravan Kismet ('Fate') touring in more 'challenging' countries.

Once there, Kismet copes with footpaths, river rafting, and joins the mile-high club on a mountain pass hailed as one of the world's most dangerous roads.

'Laugh out funny and a great travel guide' and 'Armchair travel delight' are just two of Jackie's many five-star reviews on Amazon. Jackie has also received a letter from Prince Charles, an award invitation to Bucharest for Dogs 'n' Dracula, while Dog on the Rhine is a frequent Amazon Bestseller.

Each book is a stand-alone adventure, although the series is consecutive in time. Forthcoming books follow her Brexit Busting Plans beyond Europe with The Beast, a self-converted 6x4-wheel-drive army truck.

Along with New York Times bestsellers and award-winning travel writers, Jackie has also contributed to a number of successful anthologies, including one of seventeen bonus chapters included in the Travel Stories box set.

Find her books on Amazon at <u>author.to/JLambert</u>

Adventure Caravanning with Dogs Series
Year 1: Fur Babies in France – *From Wage Slaves to Living the Dream*
Dog on the Rhine – *From Rat Race to Road Trip*
Dogs 'n' Dracula – *A Road Trip Through Romania*
It Never Rains Bit It Paws – *A Road Trip Through Politics And A Pandemic*
Forthcoming:
To Hel in a Hound Cart – *Touring Poland in a Pandemic*

Adventure Travel with Dogs Series
Pups on Piste – *A Ski Season in Italy*

Anthologies
Travel Stories Series & Box Set
Itchy Feet: *Tales of travel and adventure*
Wish You Were Here: *Holiday Memories*
The Travel Stories Collection: *3 x eBook Box Set with 17 bonus chapters*

Robert Fear Anthologies
40 Life Changing Events: *2022 Edition (Memorable, Inspirational and Life Changing Stories)*
Find me on Amazon at author.to/JLambert

I would like to dedicate this book to my lovely school friend Alexandra (Alex) Horspool, nee Slinger. I still can't believe that the world has lost this funny, witty, clever, athletic, caring and acerbic treasure.

Although we have been parted by time and many miles, Alex, I miss you terribly.

PROLOGUE

"May you live in interesting times." – A Chinese proverb

All of our lives are played out against a background of world events, yet the miniscule threads of our existence seldom coincide with that gargantuan backdrop. Millions of scenarios gig along simultaneously, like performances in adjacent theatres, each insulated from the other by soundproof walls. We glimpse them only if we open the door.

Occasionally, great happenings hove into view like a sperm whale coming up for air, before diving back into the depths of its own deep-sea reality.

Mostly, we don't notice.

Sometimes, a few droplets from the splash might land upon us. They may register briefly in our consciousness, but once the sun dries them off and the ripples dissipate, the ocean's surface becomes calm once again, and order is restored.

My husband, Mark, and I have tried our best to shield ourselves from the stresses and strains of modern life.

We gave up work to travel and integrate more of what we love into our lives. We simplified and decluttered, selling most of our belongings, then fulfilled a long-held dream to share our lives with four dogs, Cavapoos Kai, Rosie, Ruby and Lani.

Our strategy generally keeps us away from the dramas that unfold in neighbouring theatres, and avoids the whale – or at least provides a sou'wester and oilskins to resist the worst of its deluges.

But occasionally, just occasionally, something strange happens. It's as if the backdrop – the benign scenery in the theatre of our lives – suddenly leaps forward and swallows us whole. The whale breaches and unleashes a tidal wave which engulfs us, and from which there is no escape.

"May you live in interesting times," is a Chinese curse, not a blessing, and we were about to discover why.

PART I

OUR EXIT BEFORE BREXIT

1. OUR EXIT BEFORE BREXIT – AN OUT OF SEASON ODYSSEY

To guarantee a clean exit from the UK, like the one Boris Johnson promised Britain from the EU, we definitely had to leave before the deadline – no ifs, no buts...

The first time Mark and I set off for Spain, there was an unprecedented heatwave. Temperatures in Iberia soared above 50°C and people died from the heat. On that occasion, we decided to turn left, and towed Caravan Kismet ('Fate') to Romania.

This time, two days before our ferry to Santander was due to depart, Mark opened an email and detonated instantly into a rant.

"I don't believe it! Our tenant has given notice!"

A short delay to redecorate, re-let and restore our income would not usually be a problem. We were nimble retirees; open to spontaneity and not terrorised by schedules. Except a huge, fanged monster called Immovable Deadline loomed over our plans. The

Three Sisters of Fate had waved their distaffs and unleashed their Furies upon us.

After toppling his predecessor, the UK had an illustrious new Prime Minister. Many refer to him as Boris, or BoJo, which I feel is somewhat informal, given his position. My innate reverence for authority demands I show him due respect. As such, I always use his full title; one befitting a Right Honourable Male Member, and call him 'The Johnson'.

Elected on a single promise to 'Get Brexit Done', The Johnson's primary Prime Ministerial proclamation determined that Britain would exit the European Union (EU) by 31st October 2019, "no ifs, no buts." He omitted to say that in the interests of serving democracy, this also meant regardless of whether it flouted any minor inconveniences, such as UK law or the will of a democratically elected parliament.[1] Famous for quoting his number of offspring as, "five or six," it was very clear; The Johnson just wasn't a detail man.

He claimed to have an 'oven-ready deal',[2] carefully prepared to tickle the EU's taste buds. The idea was simple – Britain should keep all the perks of being in the club without paying for membership. Unfortunately, if it existed at all, The Johnson's deal was still a bunch of disparate ingredients, and he didn't have a recipe. And it was all on a metal plate that would explode the second it was placed in the EU's microwave.

His assertion that he "would rather be dead in a

ditch" than extend Brexit beyond Halloween, even if it meant a No Deal Brexit,[3] concerned us.

Our quest to Live the Dream is all about a voyage of discovery. We wanted to explore Spain, then spend the winter skiing in Italy. If Britain left the EU without a deal in place, which looked increasingly likely, all agreements with the EU would be void.

Never mind the catastrophe predicted for Britain, our personal No Deal fallout would mean invalid UK pet passports – and four fur babies who could no longer travel with us to Europe.

Hence, a pressing need to make our exit before Brexit.

The 'Phew! What a scorcher!' headlines and pictures of packed beaches that accompany British heatwaves, however brief, quickly yielded to the mother of all monsoons. Gale-force winds cleared the path for ex-hurricane Lorenzo's boisterous approach to the fair shores of Blighty. With over seventy flood warnings in place across the British Isles, it could mean only one thing.

The Ca-Lamberti, as our friends call us, were back on tour!

Four years previously, when we departed on our very first road trip, cramming our life into a box on wheels was a work of art. This time, we intended to be away for a year, not a paltry three months. Our expedition would incorporate a full span of the seasons, which compelled us to find space for a few extras normally consigned to storage between junkets. This included three boxes of ski gear, four pairs of skis, a set of winter tyres for our van, Big Blue, plus the new portable caravan air conditioning system we'd purchased as indemnity against simmering Spanish temperatures. It arrived the day before we had to cancel our ferry to Spain.

To compensate for this extra baggage, we left behind the caravan awning (the tent-like extension that goes on the side) and reduced our arsenal of windsurfing equipment by a couple of boards and sails. Mark weighed everything fastidiously: we were within our weight limits.

Just!

"I've missed this!" I said to my beloved, as we lay in bed with Michael Flatley and the full cast of Riverdance practising their steps on the caravan roof.

It was the sweetest homecoming to wake once again in our wobble box, despite the relentless rain hammering down. Somehow, it makes her feel like more of a sanctuary. Caravan Kismet is our happy place.

Mark and I had chosen to close the door on the noise and bustle of modern life. Our aim was to maintain the ordered serenity of a Zen retreat within our private theatre. Yet, despite our best efforts, we were not as insulated as we thought. An overspill of chaos seeped in from the theatre next door.

Now and again, The Fates conspire to weave patterns into your destiny over which you have no control. The previous year, when tragedy struck, we cut short our ski season and hurried home.

Mark's mother and brother had gone missing. A frenzy of transcontinental phone calls to relatives, friends and the dreaded port of last resort – the emergency room – eventually revealed their whereabouts. They had both been rushed into the same hospital on the same day, for different reasons. Mark's brother, Nigel, had collapsed in the street, and his elderly mum had taken an age-related turn for the worse.

Nigel received a horrendous diagnosis; aggressive and incurable leukaemia (blood cancer). When he returned home from hospital after intensive treatment, he still needed care. With his immune system suppressed by chemotherapy, he couldn't have contact with our pups.

Living the Dream in a caravan on the front lawn of a Surrey bungalow was never in the plan, but to maintain separation, that's exactly what we did. We pushed a note through every door in the cul-de-sac to explain that we were a family in crisis, and the encampment of travelling folk on the lawn was only temporary. After that, the neighbours were very understanding.

Dumped back in the UK, our dream lifestyle morphed into endless rounds of hospital visits interspersed with dog walking and domestic chores. There was no quick fix. As winter moved into spring and beyond, we cancelled our planned summer travels to give both patients the care they needed.

We wouldn't have had it any other way; the ties of love and loyalty are immutable. Yet constraint within four walls when there is a world out there to explore is a singular form of purgatory for a perpetual nomad.

Sadly, Mark's mum passed away aged 96, but his brother made a miraculous recovery. He is now completely clear of cancer, which proves there is always hope!

With our lives back on track, we planned and packed, and just as we were ready to embark on our out of season odyssey, our tenant gave notice.

Now, finally, snuggled up in our tin box with four cuddly pooches, we oozed cosiness and contentment. What followed, however, would not be the most restful few nights.

Parked at beautiful Corfe Castle in rural Dorset, the sound of tank and machine gun fire on the nearby Lulworth army ranges ceased at 10 p.m. Nevertheless, pitched beneath a majestic old oak, sleep did not come easily. Bombardment by autumn's bounty continued around the clock.

We enjoyed the full repertoire of tonality one can derive from the impact of acorn upon AluTec. As violent storms raged around us, like the tortured souls of the damned, acorns bounced along our roof like ping-pong balls. In the wee small hours, we giggled as the wind rolled them backwards and forwards in a crazy game of rooftop pinball. Occasionally, staccato cracks punctuated the rolls and bounces. It was easy to imagine Kismet was under attack by volleys of ball bearings, or navigating a perilous nocturnal course through an imaginary field of asteroids.

With such high stakes, we also found it difficult to disengage ourselves from the politics. We'd spent the summer trapped on a lawn in a caravan, then in our vacated apartment. If we didn't get our act together, we faced winter trapped in our home country.

Although Parliament passed a law to prevent a No Deal Brexit, The Johnson threatened to ignore it.[4] One thing was certain: we were in a race against time. To guarantee a clean exit from the UK, Mark and I needed to leave before the deadline. No ifs, no buts.

Political turmoil notwithstanding, the Fates had strewn a selection of small but apparently insurmountable problems in our path to hinder us.

The first, insurance, occupied a whole day. The dilemma was that we were effectively taking two trips. Six months of skiing, which required off-piste ski cover, followed by six months of summer touring around the Baltic states of Latvia, Lithuania and Estonia. Seemingly, this presented an actuarial impossibility.

"Why not just take out two policies?" I said to Mark. "Simples!"

He enlightened me with the doleful resignation of Albert Einstein tasked with explaining the concept of addition and subtraction to a benign idiot.

"That's a great idea, except that each policy must begin in the UK. As you know, there's lots to see in the Baltics, so we're launching stage two from Italy to get a head start. That's why we're towing the caravan over there for the winter, instead of coming back to collect it after skiing, like we usually do."

Our motto is that 'there is always a solution', so we settled on cover for an entire summer of off-piste skiing.

I know.

I said there is always a solution; not always a perfect solution!

Second came the van-dermonium.

Our stressometer was already approaching the red-zone when a simple question about removing Big Blue's bulkhead to expand the dog bed prompted our insurer to volunteer a vital piece of information,

"We don't insure vans."

"How odd!" Mark replied. "Since you've insured both our van and caravan for the last four years!"

The van-archy continued with our local Hyundai dealer. They had looked after Big Blue, a Hyundai iLoad, for nearly a decade. Then suddenly, they got size-ist and declared her overweight.

"We can't test that, mate! She's 3,200kg. That's 200 kg over. She needs a Category 7 MOT and we don't do those."

Mark's rant went supernova.

"Whaaat? You've sat on our booking for months! You've MOT'd this van before – and she's one of your own models! You must know the specification. She's our only vehicle and when the MOT runs out, she'll be illegal to drive. That means in a few days, we'll have no transport!"

The technician turned his back and didn't even have the decency to shrug. His unapologetic dismissal unleashed impotent wrath, and a rash of fevered appeals to MOT test centres across the entire south of England.

"Cat. 7? We've nothing for months, mate."

Persistence finally yielded a cancellation in Southampton, ninety-minutes' drive away. Despite a wheeziness in the engine department and a squeakiness about her wheels, Big Blue's mechanical check-up raised no costly catastrophes. Despite being a first-timer, she flew through her new Cat. 7 MOT.

After ten years of loyal service, her only problem was cosmetic. Mark remedied this with a rather colourful, if eclectic, application of pink flowery stickers to hold on her peeling paint. Oh, and he found another insurer.

Other than that, all we had to do was source and replace Kismet's microwave, which had gone on permanent strike, and stock up on essentials. This included a winter's-worth of porridge, and a year's supply of PG Tips tea bags.

I know the purpose of travel is to broaden the mind and embrace new and unfamiliar experiences, but like whelks, Delhi belly and sunburnt butt-cheeks, there are some things I've tried and never want to revisit. A few simple home comforts would deliver us from evil in the form of Continental muesli, adulterated with chocolate chips, and the unspeakable horror that is Yellow Label tea.

At the end of our previous trip, Mark had smashed a towing mirror. We mused that this was perhaps the source of our bad luck. Once we located the replacement, delivered in error to a farm somewhere near Corfe, we were all set to depart.

So, when the ferry company changed our sailing to a gale-free day, and allocated us a pet-friendly cabin, a new facility introduced by Brittany Ferries on their French crossings, it worried me.

Everything was going far too well...

2. THE FUR FRIENDLY FERRY TO FRANCE

We Try Brittany Ferries' New VIP (Very Important Puppy) Service

Now we're seasoned doggy drifters, with five years of waggy-tailed wanderings under our belts, people often ask, "Ferry or Eurotunnel. Which is best?"

From Bournemouth, it was always a lengthy diversion to the Channel Tunnel at Folkstone, but a swift half-hour crossing, during which the dogs stayed with us in the van, seemed worth it. However, our relationship with Eurotunnel Le Shuttle ended abruptly with a dramatic price hike on a previous trip. We had been making good progress across France, so we called to see about moving to an earlier crossing the following day.

"It's £2 to change your booking now. If you wait, it might go up a bit," the operator told us.

"It's a long drive and we're towing a caravan, so

we're not sure what time we'll arrive in Calais. We'll call when we're nearer," Mark said. We figured that even if it rose from £2 to £10, it would be worth it.

The next day; "Change your booking? Certainly, sir. That's £88.00 please."

The operator played back the recording of the previous day's telephone conversation to prove that, "it might go up a bit" constituted fair warning of a 4,500% increase to change the booking, which constituted a near doubling of the price for the crossing.

"It's much more expensive to change your reservation on the day of travel," they said, by way of justification for such daylight robbery.

We argued that it would have been more honest to have said it would "go up *a lot*", and that they could easily choose to waive the charge as a gesture of goodwill to a regular customer. Many times, we had turned up at the Tunnel early and were waved on to the next train! They still refused, so we stuck to our principles. Like Nero fiddling while Rome burned, we sat in the terminal for six hours while partly filled trains raced across the Channel. They didn't catch us out, so they lost the £88.00 – and the fare from every channel crossing we've made since. Never let it be said that the Lamberts are not tenacious about holding a grudge!

Despite the speed and convenience of the Tunnel, I still prefer the ferry. Arriving somewhere by boat is always romantic. Rather than a noisy, frantic chase through the underworld beneath *La Manche*, the relaxed ambience on board makes the journey an enjoyable part of the trip. Usually, we book an overnight sailing and have a meal and a beer, before turning in to awake refreshed in France. Our only problem is separation anxiety. We hate being apart from our pups!

Leaving our precious fur family in the familiar surroundings of the caravan during the crossing was just about bearable. However, the ordeal of our first trip, when we put them in the kennels – we thought for their own comfort – was like committing them straight into Dante's ninth circle of Hell.

The sickening stench of diesel engulfed the cramped steel cages in a corner of one of the car decks, while the roar of the ship's engines and the ungodly shriek of vehicle alarms assaulted our eardrums. Our poor little fur babies cowered and quivered with terror. It tore at our souls to abandon them to their fate. There and then, we vowed, "Never again!"

So, the pet friendly cabin was a godsend. Our fur family could stay with us during the crossing, and we even had a window and easy access to the doggie exercise deck. Luxury! Previously, we'd only ever had inside cabins with no natural light. It was a great start, although our journey was not all plain sailing.

The night before our departure, we stayed on a campsite near the ferry terminal at Portsmouth. The weather was vile and a serious accident held us up on the motorway. We had a booking, but as we looked for signs of life at 8:10 p.m. through lashing rain and in the pitch dark, the reception was deserted. Mark rang the warden's number posted on the door and was greeted with;

"Do you want the police or an ambulance?"

"Oh. I think I've got the wrong number. I am trying to contact the site warden."

"I am the site warden. I'm off duty. If you are going to arrive after 8 p.m., you should ring."

"Sorry, but we didn't know. We're ten minutes late and thought it was best just to get here. We were caught in traffic and didn't have the number to hand. There was an accident on the M27."

"Your wife could have rung."

It was going to be like that.

"We're catching the ferry from Portsmouth at 8:15 a.m., so we need to be at the terminal by 7:15 a.m. at the latest."

"We don't open the gates until 7 a.m."

Welcome!

I appreciate wardens work long hours with demanding customers and it was getting towards the end of the season. However, for twenty-five years, I worked long hours in a customer-facing role and remained helpful and polite every day of the year. That even included the day I did a six-hundred-mile round trip to deliver free training at my client's request and they didn't show. My job depended on it. I even declined politely when his colleague said, "You can come back and do the training another day, can't you?"

Mark and I made a mental note. In our experience, every campsite near the Poole ferry terminal was very flexible about gate opening times, to ensure esteemed patrons would not miss their crossings. At this point, I shall share with you my number one secret for commercial success, gleaned from my quarter century in field sales:

Meet your customers' needs.

Fail in that and you don't have a business!

At least our pitch was flat, so we didn't have to mess about with levelling blocks. Since we had no intention of leaving Kismet unattended, there was no need to fit the hitch and wheel locks, which were always a bit of a fiddle. We wound down the corner steadies, connected up the electricity, but didn't bother with the water. Then, to facilitate a hasty exit the following morning, we left the van and caravan hitched. Even this abbreviated set up left us soaked and bedraggled, but we had no comfort to hand. When we were packing, Mark had asked me,

"Is there anything you need out of the van before I put the bikes on the back?"

"No," I replied smugly, although I had failed to realise, I was down to my last two tea bags! When the full gravity of my miscalculation hit me, Mark made a ruling.

"You can't have tea until the bikes come off!" – so who needed water?!

It wasn't just the relentless thrashing of rain that kept me awake. The persistent gremlin of dread invaded my dreams, although our 7 a.m. start went better than expected.

My first concern; whether we could get the caravan off the sodden pitch, was fine. My second was that to press home the significance of ten minutes, the miserable warden would deliberately delay us by opening the gates late. This fear was assuaged at six forty-seven. I wound down my window to thank her, but she turned her back and ignored me, which says much more about her than me. We would not be back.

With seconds to spare, we screeched to a halt alongside the check-in booth. As usual, the staff scanned The Fab Four's microchips, but for the first time, we had to show their muzzles. On-board, we treated ourselves to a final full English breakfast in our cabin, had a long, hot shower, followed by a lovely restful sleep on cool sheets, starched to a crisp. We interrupted our slumber to make a few unsuccessful trips to the exercise deck. The Pawsome Foursome didn't seem to understand that the metal-floored area, supplied with a bin and a hose, was for peeing and pooing, so nobody did.

For the last few days, I had been asking Mark, "Are you excited yet?"

He always replied, "Not until we're on the ferry."

As the boat docked in France, we sat in the van, ready to disembark. As the ramps dropped, brilliant shafts of sunlight stabbed into the dark interior, and opened a dazzling portal through to a new adventure. Finally, I got the answer I had awaited.

"NOW I'm excited!"

Contrary to the forecast, the weather in Ouistreham, the port at Caen, was mild and pleasant as we queued to exit. The delay was caused by the novel experience of having our passports scanned; a preparatory exercise for Brexit. I quietly hoped practice would make perfect, since, despite being one of the first to disembark from a ferry that was barely half full, it took us nearly an hour to clear customs.

The weather predicted by the forecast came later. A furious storm illuminated our route towards Alençon and Radon with a mixture of bolt and sheet lightning. Curiously, the volume was on mute as we meandered through pretty, mountain scenery. This was a bonus for our black-and-white girl, Rosie, who is cool with most things, but terrified of thunder.

A mosaic of autumnal trees and russet ferns decorated the bends as we twisted through the Forêt d'Écouves and the Normandie-Maine Regional Natural Park. We decided not to push on too far, since although we'd foiled Brexit, that wasn't the only deadline on our minds.

30th September and 15th October are magical dates on the French camping calendar. After that, most campsites close for the season. It was nearing the end of October, so we didn't want to arrive late in the evening, only to find our proposed campsite closed and no alternatives nearby.

Although we had stayed there a couple of years ago, Mark claimed no memory of Camping Écouves in Radon, Normandy. As we pulled up in saturating rain, my recollection of the pitches being mostly grass was confirmed. My heart sank more swiftly than a caravan in a quagmire. Thankfully, Madame found us a small area of hard-standing, which saved me the worry of becoming too submerged in French culture on our first night.

As I took the pups for a waterlogged woodland walk, and a much-needed canine call of nature, I was elated. I performed a mental fist pump. I thought to myself,

It never rains but it pours, but in spite of everything that's gone wrong, we've done it! We've actually set off...

It was too late to go via Spain, but we could still take the slow road to our ski season in our beloved Italy. After being grounded for eight months by nursing responsibilities, followed by several false starts, each doomed by problems arising days before departure, we were finally back on tour!

3. HINTS ON HEATING, HEROINES & HORSES – RADON TO JARGEAU

A Drive through Le Perche towards Orléans; we run into lots of problems – and run out of tea!

I was gagging for a cuppa!

My last tea bag was long gone and all other supplies were buried somewhere in Big Blue. Mark was immovable and reiterated his point,

"No foraging 'til the bikes come off!"

Since we planned a succession of brief, one-night stops to make headway away from the endless rain, I feared that might yet be some time.

If you wondered which route we selected to travel south, we were very much under the radar. By that, I mean the French meteorological radar map, which traced our movements exactly with a biblical rain-storm straight down the centre of the country. If you wondered about our re-route to avoid the rain, we remained resolutely under the radar. A few days later, there was no mistaking it. The deluge was following us!

Sometimes, Ruby, our little red girl, likes to greet the day with a song. It is an occasional morning ritual, only ever initiated by Ruby, who decided our soggy overnight in Radon warranted a pack howl.

As top dogs, Mark and I feel it's only good etiquette to join in. Although we had no neighbours on this occasion, I sometimes wonder if our synchronised singing has ever had an audience. Before you question the sanity of two humans howling hearty accompaniment to a Cavapoo quartet, I must assure you our pups are not early risers. I also recommend you try it. Never mind an egg, go to work on a howl. It's highly therapeutic!

Ruby was clearly the first to recognise the morning was a cause for celebration. The previous day's downpours and storms had given way to a dry, warm, and even slightly sunny backdrop for our drive through the French region of Le Perche in southern Normandy.

It took me a while to realise this was THE Le Perche; home of the magnificent Percheron heavy horse; cover child of my *Observer's Book of Horses and Ponies* when I was an equine-obsessed eight-year-old. Despite careful scrutiny, the only example of 'the noblest, absolutely most gorgeous horses in the world'[1] was a giant green resin model on a roundabout. I can't say it did the breed justice.

The landscape, however, led me to understand how Colette Rossant, a New York Times journalist, was so smitten on her first visit that she bought a house there within three days![1]

Glorious, medieval towns, such as Bellevilliers and Bellême, which perches atop the crest of a hill, peppered the picturesque, rural scenery of Le Perche. With Caravan Kismet in tow, we couldn't stop to explore, but we admired each town as we drove through. That is why we much prefer to avoid the toll roads, which speed you past France's hidden bucolic glory. We agreed to add the entire region to our burgeoning list of 'places we must come back to'.

Luckily, in my *Camellia sinensis* deprived state, I didn't know Bellême was home to a tea room serving more than twenty types of tea. Lucky too that, as a life-long equine-obsessive, I was blissfully unaware of a nearby farm where Laurent Renou bred Percherons. Otherwise, I too might never have left!

As we passed out of the pastoral perfection of Le Perche, the scenery levelled into France's flat larder of monoculture.

Our destination, Jargeau, was not a metropolis. Most of its attractions on Trip Advisor were elsewhere, but it did have one important attribute – a campsite that was open. Its other claim to fame was that *Jeanne d'Arc* (Joan of Arc) was wounded there while fighting off the English on 12th June 1429.

On first impressions, the campground seemed idyllic; right on the banks of the River Loire and within walking distance of the town. The pitch was grass, although it didn't seem wet enough to trigger my immersion anguish.

Mark and I have a well-established routine to set up camp. While he does all the easy stuff, like levelling, locking, winding down the caravan legs, unloading the van, collecting water and connecting up the electricity, I walk the dogs.

Jeanne d'Arc said, "Go forward bravely. Fear nothing," so I took the pups along the beach next to the Loire. Never mind the terror of a bogged down caravan, or the risk of drowning in France's longest river, the worst hazard was the plants. As The Pawsome Foursome raced through scrubby vegetation on the riverbank, hundreds of small sticky burrs embedded in their coats. I had to stop every few minutes to tease them out, to prevent them from matting too deeply into their fur.

The absolute highlight was Lani scooting her backside straight over a heap of burrs that I had just extracted from Rosie. By the end of the walk, the tips of my fingers were sore and tingling, as though I had been to a petting zoo dedicated to those hairy caterpillars your mum always told you not to touch.

I felt a pressing disagreement with Miss d'Arc, who claimed, "All battles are first won or lost in the mind."

Not, perhaps, when you're dealing with sticky burrs and a dog's bum.

Later, Mark and I strolled into town, where a statue depicts Joan, France's national heroine, holding her hand to the wound on her forehead. She attacked and captured the fortress at Jargeau just after her tremendous victory against the English at Orléans.

Although his father had died five years before, the dauphin, Charles, was still not confirmed King of France. This led to a rival claim from Henry VI, the Lancastrian King of England, allied with Philip the Good, Duke of Burgundy. Between them, they tried to conquer France as part of the Hundred Years War.

For months, the Anglo-Burgundian forces had besieged Orléans but in May 1429, within nine days, the seventeen-year-old *Pucelle d'Orléans* (Maid of Orléans) broke the siege. She also broke the spell of invincibility that had persisted since the English crushed the French at Agincourt in 1415.

Subsequently, Joan ran a brave and successful campaign, which led to the dauphin's coronation as King Charles VII of France in Reims, on 17th July, 1429.

A year later, at Compiègne, as she protected her rear guard on a river crossing, the English unhorsed and captured the Maid of Orléans. Since Charles VII, the very king she had put on the throne, was now busy negotiating a truce with Duke Phil *le Bon*, he did nothing to save her.

Famously, her captors imprisoned the pious Jeanne, whose standard bore an image of Christ in judgement, and tried her as a heretic. Obviously, the church disapproved of her claims that she was in direct communication with God; that was *their* job. Plus, discrediting a French king enthroned because of witchcraft did no harm to Henry's rival cause.

But even worse, a teenage peasant girl whipping the mighty ass of England was more than a little embarrassing.

The trial was manifestly unfair. Joan's enemies presided over it and permitted her no defence. She was burned at the stake in Rouen on 30th May, 1431. True to her unwavering faith, this remarkable nineteen-year-old exhorted a priest to hold high a crucifix so that she might see it above the flames.

The Hundred Years War against the English continued for two decades after Joan's death, ending when Philip of Burgundy defected back to the French cause under the Treaty of Arras. Nevertheless, *Jeanne d'Arc* remains a heroine in the French consciousness. Militarily, the siege of Orléans was a turning point in the war, but more importantly, her faith, courage and strength in the face of overwhelming odds remain so inspiring that they ring down the centuries.

It took twenty years for King Charlie Boy to remember his loyalties and order an inquiry into Joan's trial. A mere quarter century after her death, Pope Calixtus III revoked the sentence; somewhat after-the-fact, particularly since the English had burned her body twice after her execution to prevent any relics from gaining a following.

Half a millennium later, in 1920, Catholic Pope Benedict XV canonised Joan, and the French parliament declared the second Sunday in May a national festival in honour of *Sainte Jeanne*.

Every year on 30th May, even the Church of England commemorates Saint Joan.

As we passed the 12th-century church of St. Etienne, soft choral music filled the soaring, vaulted ceilings. For the first time, I was transported into the realm of heavenliness that the cathedral builders aimed to re-create on earth. At least it helped dispel my ear worm; *Joan of Arc (Maid of Orléans)* by the band Orchestral Manoeuvres in the Dark.

We fancied a beer, but honoured our commitment to Go Sober For October when we failed to find an open bar. It was not fair. With my supplies of PG Tips buried somewhere in Big Blue, I couldn't even claim to be tea total!

As we meandered back through the cobbled streets, a vivid rainbow framed the vista and reflected in the Loire. Mark and I engaged in a team discussion. Although Jargeau was close to the Forêt d'Orléans, we didn't love the campsite – or the burr-filled river walk – and decided to hit the road. After all the thunderous precipitation, Kismet's entire contents were coated with a damp blend of various French soil types. The joys of wet-weather caravanning with four mucky pups in the mix pressed home the urgent need for an appointment with a launderette.

Then, with that impeccable sense of timing that all heating systems reserve for vicious cold-snaps and Christmas Day, Kismet's Alde boiler packed in. The error message flashed up too briefly to read, although repeated quick glimpses eventually led to a diagnosis of an 'Alde overheat red fail'. The manual suggested bleeding air from the system and checking the fluid level in the expansion tank, so we topped up the tank with a little fluid (oooh!) but thankfully didn't need to bleed the air (ahhhh!). We checked the circulation pump was responding and, as per instruction, waited fifteen minutes for the fluid to cool down – and nothing happened.

So, we resorted to the Holy Grail of Hindispensible Honline Hints – YouTube. A six-minute home video of the mighty ass of England, clad in leggings, burrowing beneath caravan sofa cushions, yielded a five-second nugget of precious information; disconnect the 12V cables from the boiler and it will reset.

And so it was that we and our soggy doggies returned from our reverie of French horses and heroines to the wonderful world of hot water and heating!

4. THE MAGIC OF MORVAN –
JARGEAU TO VÉZELAY, BOURGOGNE

*We explore the magical, medieval bastions of Burgundy –
and finally drink some tea...*

"You're a sweetie. You're my gorgeous girl. I love you soooo much!" crooned Mark.

"What would you like me to do?" On hearing Mark's voice, the harsh electronic monotone of the satnav scythed across the tender moment.

"Shut up. I'm talking to Lani!"

Curiously, that was the last that we heard from the satnav's spurious and unpredictable voice-activation. Upstaged by a dog in Mark's affections, she decided to punish us. As a result, we missed several turns, although blame did not fall entirely on the Silence of the Satnav. As I gossiped away to pass the time, Lani wasn't the only one upon whom my beloved bestowed his tender words. He crooned softly to me,

"I've said before that you're blind and deaf, but you do make up for it by not being dumb..."

"So much for trying to keep your other half informed and entertained on a long journey!" I exclaimed.

I responded further via the incontrovertible method of having an indirect dig at your partner through the medium of a conversation with a child or pet, which infers their full agreement with your stance.

"Dad's a b****** Lani, isn't he? He's cruisin' for a bruisin', although, he does have a point. Because I never shut up, my parents did always say, 'You're never alone with a Jackie...!'"

A slow start saw us leave Jargeau at around 11:30 a.m. A scenic drive along the River Loire followed part of the *Circuit des Mariniers de Loire*. This route explores the historic backdrop of the water folk who used the river to trade, and who played a vital role in the rise of Paris and Orléans.

As we moved away from the river, a clear pale-blue sky spread over an expansive agricultural landscape, chequered in earthy tones of dark brown and chestnut, with highlights of parrot green. Some of the roads were very narrow and 'interesting'. Had we been in Romania, the Route de Clamecy, which snaked up and down through a forest, would have raised a few concerns. In

Dracula country, such roads tend to peter out unexpectedly – or turn into footpaths. Extreme fun when towing a seven-metre caravan! Thankfully, in France, *la route* remained both paved and passable to vehicles.

I snapped photographs of the commune of Gien-sur-Loire, the pretty church at Faverelles, and the picturesque town of Saint-Amand-en-Puisaye. The villages of Sully and Clamecy looked very gorgeous, and we lamented that we would miss Sunday's *Fête de la Pomme* in Billy-sur-Oisy. Who doesn't love an apple festival in a town called Bill?

The village of Limon had a strange affection for decorated plastic garden chairs. Resplendent with coats of bright paint, applique, or flags, some stood unceremoniously outside houses. Others had pride of place, secured halfway up a lamppost, or suspended from a tree. Sadly, my camera battery died just in time to deny me a photo of both the dangling deckchairs of Limon, and Clamecy's ancient windmill.

In the famous wine region of *Bourgogne* (Burgundy) and nestled on the northern edge of the *Parc Naturel Régional de Morvan*, our destination was Vézelay. Its Benedictine Abbey has World Heritage status, while the place itself is deemed 'one of the most beautiful villages in France'. Being close enough to Avallon for there to be road signs, it inevitably started me up with a Roxy Music-based ear worm.

Our first view of Vézelay was a hill that looked like a celebration cake, iced with magnificent medieval buildings. Unfortunately, scaffolding covered two of the most prominent ones, although as we drove through the steep cobbled streets, age-old facades oozed charm and the aura of centuries past.

Since Camping de l'Ermitage was deserted and its reception closed until 4 p.m., we selected our own pitch. In keeping with tradition, I left Mark to his chores and took the pooches for a romp. We followed a little farm track uphill to the outskirts of Vézelay. There, the ancient gnarled vineyards presented me with no alternative. My only choice of outlook was the breathtaking view of the village atop its 'Eternal Hill'.

When he arrived at 4 p.m., Kula, the receptionist, introduced himself in perfect English. Map boards outside the site tempted us with a plethora of beautiful walks around the village. I was also excited to learn that we were just an hour away from Guédelon Castle, which had long been on our wish list. If you are not familiar with Guédelon, it is a fantastically daring feat of experimental archaeology; a medieval castle being built using only traditional methods.

Guédelon featured on the BBC2 documentary *Secrets of the Castle*. In the series, historian Ruth Goodman and archaeologists Peter Ginn and Tom Pinfold live and work as medieval builders to explore the lifestyle and skills of the period. Even better, I noted that Guédelon was open until 3rd November and was dog friendly. The Fab Four could visit if they stayed on their leads.

Kula told me they modelled Guédelon on its neighbour, Château de Saint-Fargeau, which was also close to a lake. His other recommendation was a forty-five-minute drive to Noyers-Sur-Serein, another of 'the most beautiful villages in France'. I reckoned it had to be phenomenal, because in the beauty stakes, even unrated French villages set the bar very high.

I had a funny feeling we might need longer than three nights.

On Mark's assurance of continuing good weather, we unleashed our portable washing machine on the caravan's damp and mud-caked contents. Mark cracked on with getting some laundry done so we could put it out to dry first thing the following morning. I cracked on with researching Guédelon and the local area – and making a longed-for cup of tea.

The bikes were off the back of the van. At last, I could access my PG Tips!

A final check of the *Meteo* before bed revealed our weather window was actually a bank of stormy cloud that was forecast to hover above us like a menacing grey halo for the next five days.

Surrounded by a mountain of wet clothes and with designs on walks and castles, this was not good news.

Although, at least with the laundry done, our day would be completely free to enjoy it!

5. WINE AND WONDER ON A WET THURSDAY – NOYERS-SUR-SEREIN, BOURGOGNE

We play satnav roulette & discover the inspiration behind Disney's Beauty and the Beast

Rain pounded on the caravan roof. Nevertheless, taking in our view across the mist-shrouded rolling hills of Bourgogne, we felt relaxed and snug: cuddled up with a coffee and four warm, sleepy puppies.

We had no internet. On the road, we get online by tethering our laptops to an internet hotspot on our mobile phone. The day before, the signal had been poor, but the rain ensured zero service, and the camp-site's free Wi-Fi was completely dead. The tragedy of being cut off like that on a wet Thursday frustrated my attempts to find a launderette to address our own mist-shrouded hills of wet laundry, steaming away gently upon every surface in the caravan.

In the spirit of 'There's no such thing as bad weather – only the wrong clothing', we embarked on an exploration of Noyers-sur-Serein dressed as the walking waterproofs. A medieval village, and as afore-mentioned, one of the 'most beautiful villages in France', Noyers is reputedly also the inspiration behind the setting for Disney's film, *Beauty and the Beast*.

Vacating the caravan for the day meant I could crank up the heating in the hope that at least some of the laundry might dry. Suddenly, leaving the awning behind didn't seem like such a good idea, although once we reached the Alps, winter wheels and snow chains would be more useful than a canvas-covered space to dry towels.

Satnav roulette adds a frisson of interest to travel. Different route options can lead to fantastic journeys of discovery. We selected 'Shortest Route', which avoided all the main roads – and treated us to gorgeous countryside and magical villages.

The Bourgogne is one of France's great viticultural areas, best known for its red and white Burgundies, made from Pinot Noir and Chardonnay grapes, respec-tively. The famous wine town of Chablis was close by, although continually passing signs for Avallon granted me no respite from my Roxy Music ear worm. However, The Cure Valley lent occasional post-punk variety, and my razor-sharp wit contributed some lead-singer-of-Roxy-Music-based humour,

"What if Isla St. Clair married Barry White, then divorced him and married Bryan Ferry? Her name would be Isla White Ferry!"[1]

Mark gave me one of his looks.

I deciphered a sign in French, which I hoped permitted us to park just outside the arched stone gateway that led into Noyers-sur-Serein. A beeline for the tourist information yielded the first joyful surprise of our visit; it welcomed dogs, and was hosting an exhibition of textiles by Marie-Thérèse Rjewsky.

Marie-Thérèse, a small, grey-haired lady with the kindest face, talked us through her art. She created colourful tapestries from recycled fabrics, quilted together into bright but meaningful montages. Like any great artworks, you could stare at them for hours and still tease out something new in the shapes, colours or tiny, hidden patterns in the fabric. She showed us *Le Oiseau Rare* (The Rare Bird), made from a much-loved 50-year-old Danish scarf. The Rare Bird, she told us, represented her husband; smaller versions of the same bird featured in many of her works.

After this wonderful artistic encounter, with information leaflets in hand, we stepped out into the square. A huddle of ancient timber-framed buildings with steep triangular gables lined the streets. Their soft edges and leaning, higgledy-piggledy arrangement was already cartoon-like. They reminded me of gingerbread houses. I could just imagine them in *Beauty and the Beast*!

The River Serein encircled the town in a watery embrace. A damp walk along its banks gave us a different view of the ancient architecture. Since the road was open only to residents, it was quiet enough to let the dogs run free. Although it is a small community, Noyers has seventy-eight classified historic monuments.

We turned left and climbed up three-hundred steep steps through a forest. This led to the ruined castle on a bluff overlooking the village. The woodland fizzed with moisture and crystalline raindrops dripped heavily off leaves. As we puffed uphill, they offered a brief cooling respite when they exploded onto our heads or trickled down our necks. The deserted ruins were hidden behind mist and mossy twisted oaks, which added to the mystical atmosphere.

A sign proclaimed three marked walks around the remains of the fortress. We took *Le Rond des Miles*, in which Georges, a caricature of the castle guardian, gave us an insight into its history via a series of information boards. The route followed the perimeter of the enormous site, which covers eight hectares – approximately eight football fields. Even in the gloom, views of the fairy-tale village below were stupendous.

In its heyday during the sixteenth century, Château de Noyers had twenty-seven towers and five drawbridges. Its downfall, however, did not come in battle.

Its final incumbent, Antoine du Prat, Baron de Vitteaux, sneaked in and installed himself in the castle by nefarious means. At that time, many Catholics questioned the legitimacy of Henri de Navarre, who became King Henry IV of France. Once established in one of the most powerful and impregnable strongholds in the country, Monsieur du Prat got a bit too big for his boots. He used the castle to plunder the area and challenge the king. To help you understand the impact of Barons behaving badly, word on the street in Noyers was, "God keep us from fire, water and Baron de Vitteaux."[2]

In 1599, Henry IV ordered the chateau to be razed, to prevent any other belligerent barons from exploiting it to oppose the crown. Fed up with de Vitteaux's abuse of his powers, villagers were willing helpers in decommissioning the castle. They happily plundered stone and tiles to repurpose as building materials for the village.

As we continued our walk, giant, outlandish faces started to loom through the mist. We had stumbled upon another of the marked routes; *Le Cour d'Artistes* – The Artist's Court. Sculptors from all over France gather annually at the castle for *Gargouillosium* – a three-day challenge to create your best gargoyle from your allocated block of rock.

The path took us past several monumental pieces of stonework. Traditionally, gargoyles played the part of guardians, whose grotesque features would dispel evil. However, their practical secondary function was to expel dirty water, which was also seen as a symbol of purification. This functionality sets them apart from purely decorative stone figures known as 'chimera'.

The term 'gargoyle' derives from the old French word *gargoule*, meaning 'throat'. Their name probably comes from the sound made by water gurgling from their mouths.

After looking around some of the workshops to the front of a few reconstructed towers, we left the third route, *L'Arbour & Sens* – a sensory excursion through the castle gardens, for another visit. Our pups were soaked after running through the wet forest, and our tiniest little girl, Lani, was shivering. A hot drink and warm surroundings beckoned.

The three-hundred step descent gave me a severe attack of 'disco leg', although my shaking shanks got me to the interim stop of the butcher's shop. Inside, an absolute cornucopia of deliciousness tantalised from every angle. Its counters overflowed with temptation in the form of patisserie, charcuterie and preserves.

Author Doug Larson once said, "Never doubt the courage of the French. They were the ones who discovered snails are edible."[3] Tureens full of glutinous gastropods suggested that 'Wall Fish' were a popular local delicacy. I don't dismiss any foodstuff I've not tried, so if you're wondering, eating *un escargot* is exactly as you would imagine; a rubbery sensation more than a taste, made palatable by a lake of garlic butter, which at least eases them down. Frogs' legs are similar – and neither taste like chicken. Nevertheless, I would put both well ahead of whelks.

I settled for two succulent Limousin steaks. From outside the open door, where Mark was restraining an enthusiastic quartet of canines, he urged me to add some casserole beef.

"There's none on display and I don't know how to ask for it!" I hissed.

"*Casserole* is a French word!" he argued back with infuriating logic.

I solved the problem by asking for, "*Du boeuf pour le boeuf Bourguignon*" – some beef for a beef Bourguignon, another famous local delicacy.

It was well past lunchtime and besides barracking my language skills from beyond the butcher's threshold, Mark urged me to, "Get some pies in case the café goes wrong."

The café did indeed go wrong. We repaired to La Faubourg, which the tourist office had assured us was dog friendly. In the warm, steamy interior, we asked if we could have a sandwich.

"*Non.*"

Scanning the menu suggested we would be good for a platter of snails, but not much else in the way of sustenance, so we opted just for coffee.

We chatted with a French lady at the next table, who had lived all over the world. Reading between the lines, we suspected her hubby was possibly a diplomat. She had recently moved to Senegal, but had spent time in London, Ireland and Sweden, to name a few.

"We had planned to settle in London, but with Brexit that looks unlikely."

Ah, Brexit. The gift that keeps giving.

Since we were in Burgundy, a wine region of great

repute, with more AOCs *(Appelations d'Origine Contrôlée[4])* than any other French *terroir*, there was only one way to finish the day; Kula, the campsite receptionist, gave us the key for the tumble dryer.

Oh, and we shared a bottle of Pinot Noir with our wonderful Limousin steak...

The perfect end to a perfect day!

6. VÉZELAY TO LES ABRETS, ISÈRE

Vents Violents, The Beautiful Village & The Eternal Hill

A wet morning gave way to a better afternoon – and the opportunity to explore the medieval streets of Vézelay.

In times past, Vézelay was a sacred place of pilgrimage. The Benedictines founded their abbey there in the 9th century, while the magnificent 12th-Century basilica, which crowns the summit of the Eternal Hill, takes its name from the relics of St. Mary Magdalene, which are reputedly held within.

Over the centuries, miracles attributed to the relics drew pilgrims to Vézelay, a place so holy it was associated with the start of both the Second and Third Crusade. It also marks the beginning of The Vézelay Way, one of the four routes of pilgrimage through France to the famous shrine of St. James at Santiago de

Compostela. In 1979, its outstanding Romanesque architecture led to UNESCO World Heritage listing.

Today's Vézelay attracts lovers of wine as well as culture. In 2017, the region's dry chardonnays earned their own designation, AOC Vézelay. This recognises their unique character and sets them apart from your generic white *Bourgogne* (Burgundy).

A twenty-minute walk from the campsite through the vineyards took us into the heart of Vézelay's maze of quaint, cobbled streets. We stopped in the tourist office to buy walking maps of the area. The smart lady in charge taunted us with her view of Brexit. With a mixture of one third bemusement and two thirds overt glee, she gloated,

"Now, you British will be prisoners in your own country!"

"It's not what *we* voted for," we assured her. "It will certainly make our travelling lifestyle more difficult."

"Prisoners in your own country!" she scoffed periodically, as we wandered around the office, collecting leaflets.

She was not wrong, but at least we'd skipped the first potential pitfall by escaping before Brexit could imprison our pups.

Tourist maps in hand, we continued uphill past gorgeous, well-preserved 15th and 16th-Century buildings. We explored a few of the narrow medieval streets, and peered into elegant courtyards. Stately trees fringed the gardens surrounding the Benedictine abbey and basilica. Like a lawned infinity pool, they looked out on to long-distance views over the Morvan and Cure valleys.

Extensive renovation work denied us a view of the basilica's renowned Central Portal, but the soaring nave was certainly built on a scale to impress. One almost miraculous detail sums up the knowledge and vision of the medieval architects. At noon on the summer solstice, nine pools of sunlight fall into the centre of the church through carefully placed roof lights to illuminate a path to the altar.

On our way back, we bought a Vézelay cake, made with almond and *cassis* (blackcurrant). It was tasty, but for me, not quite on a par with a Mr. Kipling's Cherry Bakewell. A honey gingerbread, typical of the area, was much dryer than expected, but captured the sumptuousness and every floral nuance of the honey. It was the perfect foil for a lovely, lovely cuppa; a luxury I now revelled in, following the serendipitous reunion with my supplies of PG Tips!

The weather forecast did not bode well for putting our walking maps to good use, so Mark and I decided to cut our losses and head east towards Italy, our ultimate destination for the winter.

Toll roads shortened our crossing of South East France by two hours, but quickly ate through €50. Even so, it was still a long and difficult drive through lashing rain. Having been told to shut up on our previous outing together, the satnav was sulking. She had sent us to Coventry permanently, so we had to be extra vigilant at junctions. Mark tried to find an interim stop to shorten the journey, but it was late October, and every campsite en route was closed for the season.

Along the motorway, illuminated gantries warned of *Vents Violents* (Strong Winds); always a concern when towing a caravan. However, the signs did not explain when, where or how bad, which was unnerving. A town called Ars lightened my spirits briefly and, despite the damp, grey backdrop, Burgundy's vineyards criss-crossed the hills with a vivid patchwork of yellow, gold and red.

Our campsite for the night was Le Coin Tranquille (The Tranquil Corner), in the Isère department of the Rhône-Alpes, near the BIG mountains. In a brief dry spell, I gave the pups a leg stretch in a field at the end of the site. When the rain returned with vengeance, I speed-squelched back to the caravan. However, I still felt a flutter of raw excitement. Jagged behemoths blocked the horizon. The primal energy of the mist-swathed Alpine peaks that surrounded us stirred my soul.

I asked whether dogs were allowed in the restaurant and checked in, all in French. On the back of this mighty linguistic triumph, we treated ourselves to a night out; *tartiflette* (oven-baked potatoes with cheese, onion and bacon) and two litres of beer. We failed to realise that the beer didn't come in a jug for sharing, and ended up with two litres each!

In our twenty-first year of marriage, I felt very blessed that Date Night with me darlin' was as special as when we first met. The pups behaved impeccably.

The *tartiflette* came with a plate of charcuterie, which both Ruby and Kai resisted, even though their noses were just inches from all those tempting treats as they curled up on our laps through dinner.

The *vents violents* made themselves apparent in the wee small hours. Scared puppies snuggled in as the raging storm turned the caravan into a giant cocktail shaker. At 8 a.m., after a restless night, I checked the *Meteo,* the French weather site, and laid out my conclusions to Mark. Severe weather warnings obliterated the entire map of the region.

My husband often accuses me of being over-cautious, and views gale-force winds as an adrenaline-infused towing challenge. I am less enamoured with the thrill of potentially overturning our home and losing all our worldly possessions, not to mention our lives. Thankfully for my emotional wellbeing, on this occasion, Mark concurred; it would be wise not to move.

The morning was surprisingly pleasant; fine but windy. In laundry terms, a good drying day! Autumn caravanning, particularly with dogs, is an eternal prison sentence of mud and wet clothing. It was a relief to do more washing and get the caravan clean and dry.

There were few options to walk straight from the campsite. We had intended to stay for just one night, so we had left Big Blue and Kismet hitched for a quick getaway and didn't want to drive anywhere. Some small, forested hills nearby looked inviting, so we set off towards the village of Les Arbrets.

The sharp report of gunshots echoed across the valley, providing a timely reminder of *La Chasse.* Hunting season, a great French tradition, is best given a wide berth by both humans and pets. From September to March, seven days a week, Frenchmen brimming with blood lust are at large throughout the countryside, wielding firearms and laying traps. When we considered the very real possibility of being shot at or snared, we pared down our perambulatory perspectives and just let the pups burn off some steam around a small field near the campsite.

As I booked us in for an extra night, my wonderful command of French swiftly added €8 to our bill. It was punishment for successfully answering the receptionist's interrogation, *"Aimez-vous le restaurant? Vous avez quatre chiens, n'est ce pas?"* – Did you enjoy the restaurant? You have four dogs, don't you?

I felt a slight glow of triumph might have registered on her face when I was obliged to answer, *"Oui"* on both counts. However, she didn't press the issue of the €8, €2 per dog, missing from the previous night's bill.

Which left me with a conundrum.

Should I be disgruntled about the higher charge for our extra night, or content with the previous night's reduction?!

7. BAROLO OR BUST – CAMPING SOLE LANGHE, VERGNE, ITALY

A Lesson about Leccy & A Trauma in the Terroir

At 9 p.m., the gods turned their fire hoses on us. Teeming rain joined the savage winds that had battered caravan Kismet throughout the day. It was like camping beneath Niagara Falls. The violence of the gale vindicated our decision to avoid towing and stay that extra night in Les Arbrets.

By morning, Mark and I were smothered in cuddly pups; scared of the rain strafing our roof like machine gun fire. It made for a slower than intended start.

Every time I tried to get up, Ruby put her paws on my shoulders, pushed me down, and pressed her little button nose into my neck. A Cavapoo the size of a rabbit is amazingly strong, but puppy love is so endearing it's impossible to resist!

In any case, it wasn't the most alluring day to rush outdoors. The weather was so foul that it was still dark at 10 a.m. A slurping swamp the size of the Everglades had developed around Kismet's step, but things got considerably worse once we had squidged through an ocean of mud to pack everything away in the rain. For the first time in a decade, Big Blue refused to start. Her battery was completely dead.

And here was the lesson we learned about leccy (electricity). We had left Kismet and Big Blue hitched to hasten our exit, but had unexpectedly stayed a second night because of the wind. Although we had plugged the caravan into the site's electrical hookup, we didn't realise that leaving the towing electrics connected would drain Big Blue's battery.

I dripped my way into Reception and from the centre of my slowly expanding personal puddle, conveyed, *"Le voiture ne marche pas."* – The car doesn't work. The receptionist kindly dispatched a man with *les pinces* – jump leads. A new French word; one perhaps worth remembering.

Our soggy saviour appeared like an apparition out of the murk, and disappeared just as quickly the second he jump-started our engine. Once he'd administered car CPR, we were on our own.

"Don't stall. DON'T STALL!" was our mantra as we eased Big Blue and Kismet forward off the slippery pitch.

"We need to do at least fifty miles without stalling," Mark pronounced. So, the first part of the journey became like the film *Speed*; we couldn't afford to slow down or stop – and all the while, the satnav maintained her stony silence. She had really taken umbrage at being told to shut up! Fortunately, we kept the engine running and didn't make any wrong turns.

Our day was toll-tastic – our journey cost well over fifty cents per mile. We crossed into Italy via the Fréjus tunnel, which relieved us of around €60: a sum equivalent to three nights' campsite fees. The motorway tolls almost doubled that. Then, to add alligators and piranhas into our monetary mire, the service station after the tunnel charged €1.89 per litre for fuel, the most we had ever paid. Throw in €7 for a brace of microscopic coffees and two barely visible bars of chocolate and I gave up. Some days, Lady Luck simply determines you will haemorrhage money.

The rain continued to lash as we invaded Italy, so we decided to forgo another interim stop and push on to the famous wine area bordering Turin. It was Barolo or Bust!

At least the barrage stopped as we progressed eastwards and entered the UNESCO-listed landscape of the Langhe in Piedmont. Its signature regiments of bosomy hills, many crowned with castles, were shrouded in fog. Some say the *nebbia,* or mist common in the locality, gives the Nebbiolo grape its name, although the 'mist' might also refer to a whitish bloom on the fruit itself. The noble Nebbiolo is used to make Barolo, the most prominent wine of the region, and reputedly one of the best reds in the world.

The chap on reception at Camping Sole Langhe in

Vergne greeted us warmly. "I lived in Wimbledon for two years!" explained his fluent grasp of English.

When we asked where we could exercise The Fab Four, he said,

"From the campground, you can walk through the vineyards to the villages of Barolo and La Morra."

While Mark made camp, I tried out one of these routes with the dogs. It didn't go well.

As I wandered away from the campsite, the sugary alcoholic scent of fermentation hung in the air. The harvest had just finished and a few partial bunches of shiny succulent black grapes still hung on the vines. They looked so perfect, I tasted one; it was delicate, sweet and fragrant. I picked a small bunch to take back for Mark.

It was warm enough to wear shorts and sandals, although my sartorial choices turned out to be unwise. The mud was unbelievable. Heavy machinery had recently passed through for the harvest and the thick, clay soil of the *terroir*, which gives the wine its body and character, stuck to my soles. With every step, they collected a further rim of clag and got heavier and heavier. It was like wearing concrete snow-shoes.

The signs on the footpath towards Barolo petered out. Half an hour later, I spotted the ochre-coloured walls and cylindrical turret of the 11th-Century Castello della Volta on its peak above Barolo, but felt I had walked far enough. I U-turned at a small lake to head back along the same path, but somehow, I strayed horribly off track. I don't know how I got it so wrong, but I felt lost at sea. Vineyards on their hills rose and fell around me like monstrous waves, making it impossible to see where I was; I was drowning in the landscape.

As the light started to fade, a tight knot of panic began unravel in the pit of my stomach. Following the trail I thought led towards our home village, I saw a sign for Vergne pointing back the way I had just come. Every crossroad was devoid of signposts. Then I slipped and fell on the slimy mud, adding insult to injury with an inelegant slither on my backside down a miry bank.

Wet and miserable, seated in a swampy ditch, I felt like a lost tear in an ocean of misery. Then, from the lowly perspective of my muddy wallow, I vaguely recognised a walnut grove I had passed as I left the campsite. I could smell fermentation. Through the trees, I saw a flash of white; a glimpse of salvation in the form of Caravan Kismet.

I snivelled, dry-sobbed and squelched my way back. I tried not to catch the eyes of our only neighbours, reading quietly outside their VW Camper. On my super-sized mud-encrusted sandals, I sidled crab-like past them to conceal my skid-marked derrière.

"I brought you some grapes. They're in a poo bag and I fell on them," I said to Mark.

He regarded my gift; a bulging doggie bag, distended with grapes and smeared with sludge from its impromptu pressing by my ample rear.

"Are you sure you haven't mixed it up with the bags containing poo?"

He noticed my chin wobble and wrapped me in a warm, protective embrace.

"It's the thought that counts."

He managed not to laugh.

And promised to clean my sandals.

Although we had been loosely following Go Sober For October, we decided that the occasion demanded wine.

It seemed incongruous to drink a French Burgundy in Barolo, one of Italy's finest wine regions, but we hadn't yet been shopping, and solace is needed when you have soiled your shorts!

8. A DOG-FRIENDLY WINE TOUR, BAROLO

Lovin' the Langhe – Land of Wine, Hazelnuts & Truffles

"How do you plan where to go on your trips?"

A good question. It's one we're often asked, although the answer is not straightforward.

I like red wine and sampled Barolo for the first time with my brother in a West London restaurant a few decades ago. It was love at first sip.

Many years later, for her 40th birthday, I spent a weekend in Turin with my best friend. Besides celebrating, I had three goals: to visit the Mole tower; to score a *Bicerin* (Turin's luscious mix of espresso and melted chocolate); and finally, to purchase a nice bottle of Barolo as a present for Mark. On my way back through the airport, I happened to pick up an attractive watercolour business card for Ca'San Ponzio, a rustic stone self-catering cottage near the village of Barolo.

Later that year, Mark and I planned our first road

trip entirely around a visit to Ca'San Ponzio. We drove to Italy, intent on enjoying the World Heritage scenery, the wonderful food and buying wine – lots of wine.

Our visit precipitated our Damascene conversion into Born Again Italians, and we returned to the area several times. As you can see, partaking of a nice bottle of red with your bro' can lead to great things – and such fickle haphazardness is how most of our trips come about.

If you want to know what is special about Barolo wine, its creation is a lengthy labour of love. DOCG (Denominazione di Origine Controllata e Garantita) is the highest designation of quality for Italian wines. Barolo DOCG must be produced from one hundred per cent Nebbiolo grapes, a finicky fruit, which needs a long season, and resolutely refuses to grow almost anywhere other than a few mist-shrouded fells in the Langhe.

Phil Collins sang, "You can't hurry love" – and the same applies to Barolo. It must be aged for at least three years, with a minimum of eighteen months spent in wooden barrels. The term 'Barolo Riserva' can only apply to wine matured for a minimum of five years. Barolo drinks best after a maturation period of ten years, and the finest vintages will keep for three decades.

Barolo wine is full bodied, intense and powerful. Usually between thirteen and fifteen per cent alcohol, its flavours range from fruity black cherries and rose petals, to leather and vanilla infused from the oak barrels. Two decades ago, as we sipped our oenological haul from oversized crystal Barolo glasses in the back garden of a semi in Woking, I remember thinking the wines Mark and I bought captured the distilled essence of rubies and Italian sunshine.

In the early noughties, Barolo's wineries welcomed us like long-lost family. They provided endless free samples of their wares in a variety of opulent wood-panelled tasting rooms. We returned home with a grossly expanded knowledge of viticulture, vintages and vineyards – and a three-hundred bottle challenge to the suspension of a Golf GTI.

On this trip, with all that meticulous research already in the bag, we retraced our steps to a few of our favourite *cantine* (cellars). The first, Rocche dei Manzoni, in the picture-perfect hill village of Monforte d'Alba, is home to a couple of very delicious wines. Barolo Big 'd Big almost punches its way out of the bottle, while its cellar mate, Vigna d'la Roul, is thinner and more austere.

The welcome was almost as warm as we remembered. The Fab Four could join us in the winery – but no tasting was available. Our youthful hostess, Alessandra, shared our enthusiasm for the Langhe, "I love the landscape and tranquillity," she told us.

Allesandra asked if our pups were truffle hounds. Alba white truffles are another world-renowned speciality of the region. At first, we thought she was joking, although we found out later that Poodles are sometimes used to hunt for 'edible gold'.

"My dog is a Lagotto Romagnolo truffle hound. My dad wants him to work, but he's really fluffy and cute. I just want him to play!"

Alessandra showed us a picture of her pooch, who looked very like our teddy-bear-faced Cavapoos. Then she showed us Manzoni's price list. We blanched a little, because the prices had more than doubled since our last visit. A bottle of 2014 Big 'd Big was nearly €60 – a Frejus tunnel crossing; or a few hundred miles of motorway tolls. With an expected storage lifetime of two to three decades, we berated ourselves for drinking every last drop we'd bought from the exceptional vintages that graced the turn of the twenty-first century. Back then, I remembered us both laughing at the idea that Barolo drank best after being cellared for at least ten years. It was a similar reaction to TV Chef Delia Smith's curious concept of freezing leftover wine in an ice cube tray, to use later in a casserole. Remind me again, what is leftover wine?

Our millennial wine collection would have been a superb investment, but when you have a cellar (garage!) full, who can resist a rejuvenating bottle of Barolo with your fish and chips after a crap Tuesday at work? And, we didn't want it all to go off because it had not been stored at the correct temperature...

We swallowed hard and treated ourselves to a couple of bottles of a slightly lesser Barolo and another local wine, Barbera d'Alba. Barbera is also full, fruity and fabulous – but considerably more benevolent to the budget.

On our way to the town of Barolo itself, we debated putting The Pawsome Foursome out to work. Alessandra told us that in 2018, two pounds of Alba white truffles sold for $85,000 – more than a Maserati Ghibli. A single season of truffle hunting might enable us to re-kindle our love affair with the venerable vini-cultural products of Piedmont.

Many past visits to the Marchesi di Barolo had put us on first-name terms with winery hostess, Maria Pia. On our second visit, Maria Pia said she remembered us. In her wonderfully romantic Italian way, she pointed at me and, in a salvo of rolling r's, proclaimed, "I-ah rememberrr yourrr-ah eyes!"

In the Marchesi's grand tasting hall, Maria Pia had plied us with her best wines, fed us local delicacies and introduced us to the village butcher and priest. Both were larger-than-life characters – and clearly regular beneficiaries of the winery's convivial hospitality. Maria Pia showed us a magazine article featuring the white-haired butcher in his thick round John Lennon glasses. He had been photographed wearing a dazzling white tunic, draped with artisan sausages, against a Damian Hirst backdrop of cleaved carcasses and choice cuts.

In a paper bag, he had brought along some wafer-thin strips of pork fat cured with herbs. By way of recommendation, Maria Pia flashed her eyes and smacked her lips, then shared them with us. She was an ample lady with jet black hair, clad in a voluminous floral spinnaker of a dress. I loved the way she dangled the glistening white ribbons of lard above her open mouth before devouring them with undisguised gusto, relishing their silky deliciousness. Concerns about calories and cholesterol will never stand between an Italian and their appreciation of first-class flavours.

Once they had both left, Maria Pia treated us to her delightful impersonation of the priest. Rolling her eyes and jabbing her thumb to indicate, "*Lui*" – him, she performed an exaggerated sign of the cross.

"*Cannubi, Sarmassa, Ruvei, Paiagal!*" she said, substituting the names of the Marchesi's best wines for "Father, Son and Holy Ghost."

It told us a lot about the priest!

Maria Pia had long since left the Marchesi, although the girls in the *cantina* remembered her. They offered no samples and left us alone to browse the shelves. They had a long table full of Japanese tourists on a paid tasting. The scruffy English couple with four dogs were clearly not worth the trouble.

Immediately, we realised our Barolo habit would not be revived at the Marchesi, either. Bottles of 2014 Barolo Cannubi or Sarmassa cost €54 each.

We lowered our sights to a couple of bottles of Barbera Paiagal and Ruvei. €16 wine was still well into the realm of 'massive treat' on our budget, although it was a compromise that granted us a bit of nostalgia without breaking the bank. A Barolo Chinato slipped into our bag. A digestif made from Barolo wine, spiced with bitter herbs and aromatics, it goes beautifully with chocolate. A necessity in the hazelnut hub that is also home to Ferrero Rocher and Nutella!

On the way back to Vergne, it started to rain. Mark and I compared thoughts on a place we had long considered one of our spiritual homes. Once, we had even contemplated moving our life out to Piedmont.

"It's so slick and commercial here now. Twenty years ago, you simply rocked up, were welcomed like beloved family, and got a free tasting. These days, you have to book in advance and pay for it!"

The girls at the Marchesi di Barolo told us it was high season. The latest vintage had just come to market, and Alba's truffle fair was in full swing. Maybe that explained why the campsite was so expensive, although Mark said that Camping Sole Langhe had only one price – and it was always high season!

We concluded that, like most things, it had been much more fun when it was all a bit rough around the edges.

Back at the caravan, I opened my email to receive some extremely upsetting news from Australia. My golden-haired school friend, Alex, had finally lost her battle against cancer. The message from her husband implored,

"Please raise a good glass of red in her memory."

I hadn't seen Alex since we left school – she had lived all over the world – but she was a constant bright light in my life. Her acerbic posts on Facebook always made me laugh, and her down-to-earth advice always made me feel better. I felt numb. Her passing left a huge crater in my heart.

Since we were in Barolo, it seemed only right to raise a glass of one of the finest reds in the world to my lovely friend.

Cheers.

9. DOGS IN BAROLO WINE MUSEUM & A TEMPLATE FOR A LONG-LOST TATTOO

Some nasty surprises as we revisit Barolo's castle!

Another question we're often asked is, "How does Mark decide on designs for his tattoos?" As with most such questions, there is an equally convoluted answer.

Mark's tattoos all have significance. Some are obvious: a Dacian wolf from Romania, wind and surf from Maui, a stylised representation of him resisting the flow of convention...

Nearly twenty years ago, on a trip around Castello Falletti in the town of Barolo, I saw a mysterious pictograph adorning a bedstead. It combined all the favourite elements of our life. Out of respect to the dimly lit antique furniture, I didn't photograph it, but regretted it ever since. The figure was Pegasus with a fish's tail; it encompassed land, air, water and horses – so much of what we love. With its connection to

Barolo, one of our spiritual homes, it would have made a perfect tattoo.

The castle in Barolo was the country home of the Falletti, a banking family from Turin, whose story is irrevocably intertwined with Barolo wine.

Although wine had been made in the Langhe for thousands of years, Giulia Falletti, the last Marchesa di Barolo, is credited with the creation of Barolo wine as we know it today. Following the death of her husband, Carlo, Giulia inherited the Falletti lands in 1838. A sharp cookie, Giulia had the bright idea of inviting oenologist, Louis Oudart, to apply the winemaking techniques of the great French vineyards to her Italian vines. And so, a viticultural star was born.

Giulia aimed high. She sent 325 barrels of her new Barolo wine to King Carlo Alberto of Savoy – one for the court to enjoy each day of the year; excluding Lent, of course. This led to Barolo's enviable branding as 'Wine of Kings – King of Wines.'

Entrance to the castle cost €8 each. The good news was the dogs could accompany us. The bad news was that the castle had also changed radically since we were last in the neighbourhood.

Our previous tour guided us through the Falletti household's domestic set up and reflected on the history of the family and the area. The castle had now transmuted into a very peculiar museum of wine. This didn't bode well for re-acquaintance with the long-lost tattoo template.

Although wine is such a joyful subject, the museum's exhibits verged on the macabre. A lift in a glass tube hurled us up to the top floor of Castello Falletti. After taking in a view across the terracotta roof tiles and vineyards of Barolo, we were drawn into a labyrinth of shadowy corridors and rooms, home to hundreds of bizarre and disturbing displays.

Among the most memorable was a crowd of life-sized, cardboard cut-outs of long-dead people. Blown up in monochrome from old sepia photographs, they all jibber-jabbered constantly through creepy LCD-screen mouths. There was a room of red light, and an 'underground' chamber with what I presume were vine roots dangling down your neck from the ceiling, like the tentacles of treacherous triffids. The 'why' behind it all was lost on me.

We narrowly avoided a dousing as we rushed through one corridor, which periodically released a soaking sheet of water from the roof. On 'The Carousel of the Seasons', I sustained an injury. A freakish contraption in a darkened circular room, it comprised a weighty six-seat wooden park bench on wheels, propelled by a multitude of bicycle pedals. It rotated to the tune of Vivaldi's *Quattro Stagioni* (Four Seasons), and fired spotlights to illuminate photographic wall murals of the Langhe at different times of year.

With Mark pedalling as fast as he could while I stood on the sidelines, holding three of the dogs, I was treated to whirling stroboscopic glimpses of a confused-looking Kai flashing past on Mark's knee every couple of seconds. A more fitting accompaniment would have been outlandish, maniacal laughter.

Then, when it was my turn to clamber aboard the rotating bench of doom in the dark, the sharp, metal pedals gouged my shin right on the bone and drew blood. Who needs a tattoo as a reminder of our visit? I still have the scar!

We kept hoping that at some point, we would enter the castle proper, but nothing of the original interior remained. It was all absurd interactive weirdness. As we descended the final staircase to the ground floor, we had abandoned hope of encountering any furnishings whatsoever, but there, right by the exit, was the bed.

I was jubilant! I had to illuminate the motif with my mobile phone, but €16 lighter, happy and bleeding, we stumbled into Castello Falletti's tasting cellar, armed with a mighty thirst, and a photograph of our long-awaited template for Mark's next tattoo.

10. THE ROAD TO GRESSONEY

Monte Rosa Ski Paradise – here we come!

Although we bought a walking map of Barolo, the vineyards were overrun with mud and mosquitoes. When the rain moved in with menaces, we made our decision to curtail our waterlogged wanderings and remove ourselves to our final destination; the tiny village of Staffal in Monte Rosa. There, we intended to spend the ski season in a cosy apartment, rather than awash with grime and condensation in a caravan.

Despite being the second highest mountain in the Alps, Monte Rosa sits incognito between her famous neighbours. The tip topmost Alp is Mont Blanc, while Matterhorn, or Cervino as the Italians call her, comes in third. For some reason, no one seems to register number two; Monte Rosa – the Pink Mountain.

'Monte Rosa Ski Paradise' spans the valleys of Champoluc, Gressoney (or Lys), and Alagna. Italy's

'Three Valleys', with 180 km of prepared slopes, is on a much smaller scale than France's vast *Trois Vallées.* The French Three Valleys boasts 600 km of piste, and claims to be the largest lift-connected ski operation in the world. However, with Monte Rosa, size isn't everything.

If you want to ski for half the price, on uncrowded slopes, beneath almost perpetual bluebird skies, Monte Rosa is an excellent choice. If you want to access a vast back country ski area, ranked as one of the best in the world, Monte Rosa is in the top five.

Geography makes Monte Rosa. Tucked away in the Aosta Valley, close to Milan and Turin, many properties are weekend retreats. This means deserted slopes during the week, or when the weekend weather is not *perfetto* (perfect). The resort villages are relatively high, between 1,191 m (Alagna) and 1,829 m (Staffal), which makes them snow sure, although most slopes have snow making facilities anyway. Located to the leeward side of Mont Blanc, Monte Rosa enjoys more than her fair share of sunshine and, being Italy, they revere food. For a fraction of the cost of a mediocre grease burger in Méribel or Courchevel, you can enjoy sensational home-cooked pasta and other delicacies in friendly and traditional mountain huts.

However, if you want raucous après-ski, go to Austria!

Monte Rosa's little-known charms mean we can stay for six months in an apartment fifty metres from the lifts without the budget of a Russian oligarch.

That fortunate situation may change, of course. There has long been talk of connecting Monte Rosa with Zermatt, a move which would vastly upstage even *Les Trois Vallées'* claims of 'We're the biggest'. Thanks to the Green movement's resistance to dynamiting a pristine wilderness, Monte Rosa is not ski paradise lost. For the moment, at least.

Driving rain accompanied us from Barolo to our campsite in Gressoney St. Jean. We followed the progression of autumn along the valley as we zigzagged up its familiar hairpins. The River Lys was higher than we'd ever seen it, fed by curtains of white water freefalling down vertiginous mountainsides.

The sun finally came out the following day, to welcome us back to our spiritual home in the mountains. It lit up a light dusting of snow on the tawny peaks above us, while the lofty Monte Rosa massif, which blocked the head of the valley, shone bright white, like a super-sized sugar loaf. When Mark killed the last Langhe mosquito to have hitched a lift with us, everything would have been perfect – had Rosie and Kai not radically altered the aroma of the a.m. by rolling in fox poo.

We popped into Gressoney St. Jean to touch base with our estate agent, Mirko. Since our apartment was empty, Mirko gave us early access. A few days later, on a beautiful golden morning, we moved in; although not without some trepidation. Not only had we never negotiated the steep hairpins above Gressoney St. Jean with a caravan in tow, we were also sketchy about where we might deposit Kismet's 7.3 metre majesty for the winter, once we arrived in Staffal.

We met Luisa, the concierge, and her small foxy-faced tricolour dog, Lampo (Lightning). Luisa was a small lady, nearing retirement, who was always immaculately attired in the latest Italian fashion. She would sport shiny puffer jackets, animal prints and angora jumpers studded with rhinestones, all set off with silver belts and handbags. She adored our dogs and, since it was our second year in the same apartment, she clasped Mark and me to her bosom while thanking us for the postcards of The Pawsome Foursome we'd sent from our travels.

The Fab Four and Lampo raced in a mad hunt around the reception area before re-acquainting themselves with a favourite Monte Rosa tradition – Luisa fed them an entire box of doggie treats. "*Ancora un giro!*" – one more round! she kept saying, giving in every time five sets of expectant puppydog eyes bored into her. Once they had devoured the first lot, she even opened a second box. With Luisa around, keeping our pack's weight under control is the winter's greatest challenge!

Kismet would not fit in the apartment's underground garage. Mark recalled a loose agreement wheedled out of the hotel manager the previous year, when we had mentioned we *might* bring along a caravan. Between Luisa, Mirko and ourselves, we reached the consensus of parking Kismet in the hotel car park, just below our apartment block.

With Kismet tucked away in a corner of the hotel car park, we took to shifting her entire contents into what would be home for the next six months. Although it took some time for the apartment to warm up after being empty since the summer, the exertion of moving our super king size memory foam mattress, Wedgewood crockery and other home comforts up four floors soon had us sweating.

Finally, we settled down with a beer to watch the original *Blade Runner* on Netflix. The film is set in the future, November 2019. We realised – that was tomorrow!

Here we were, on the eve of the future – and all the human race had to show for it was a new model Ford Mondeo.

How disappointing we didn't have flying cars. It would have made light of those hairpins – and moving home on a mountainside would have been a breeze!

PART II

MONTE ROSA SKI PARADISE

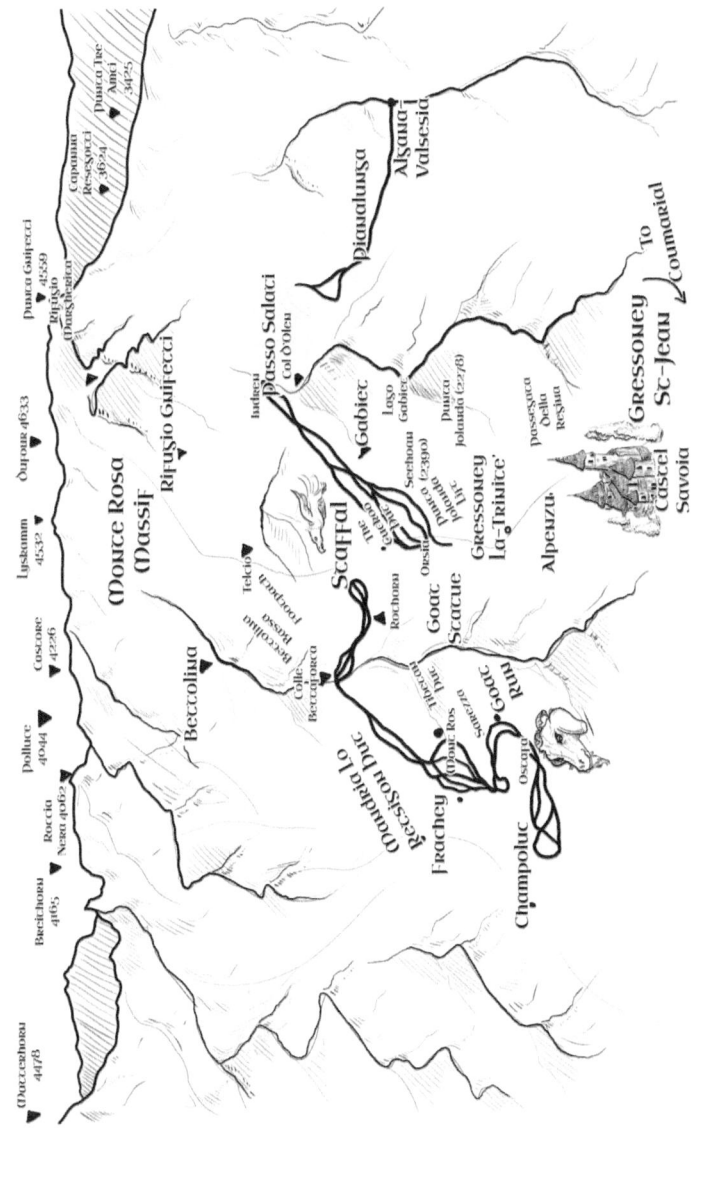

11. BACK IN THE OLD ROUTINE

We experience snow, linguistics & rapture

Halloween passed quietly. On this particular October 31st, the UK remained part of the EU, no ifs, no buts, and with no one dead in a ditch.

We'd endured muck, murk and mosquitos to escape The Johnson's immovable Brexit deadline. I read the British government had doubled its budget, and sacrificed an additional £2.1 billion of taxpayers' money to cushion the Brexit blow.[1] They splurged the cash on bolstering the border force, preparing businesses for an inundation of paperwork, and stockpiling body bags for when the NHS (National Health Service) fell over, due to shortages of medicines and staff.[2]

Protected from all that political nonsense, we settled into our winter routine. In Monte Rosa, November is a quiet, in-between time. The ski resort wouldn't open for another month, so before the first snows, we occupied ourselves with peaceful autumnal walks. On the opposite side of the River Lys from our accommodation, footpath No. 7 took us beneath the towering crags of our rocky three-thousand-metre neighbour, Punta Telcio. The path continued towards Monte Rosa, which forms the border between Italy and Switzerland.

In shorts and T-shirts, we strolled along the river in Gressoney la Trinité, accompanied by the melody of rushing water, cowbells, and the all-pervading musk of manure. Both farmers and cattle were making their final contributions to fertilising the fields in preparation for spring. Our regular walk followed Footpath No. 8, 'the zigzag', which started next door to our residence. Lampo joined us most days for a stroll up through the conifer forest from Staffal's Oagre Chapel, a dainty white oblong, dedicated to Our Lady of the Snows.

In summer, the zigzag is a rough, forest track. In winter, it is a groomed ski run called Marmotte; a tranquil alternative to the steep and busy red[3] piste from Col Bettaforca into Staffal. Marmotte is fine for winter walkies, so long as you avoid the busiest periods – such as weekends and the finishing-times for ski school. Then, crowds of out-of-control children come pelting down, cooing at the dogs rather than looking where they are going. It is a challenging climb of 328 m (1,076 ft), but always pretty, offering a wealth of viewpoints from which to drink in the visual charms of our magical valley.

The snow arrived on 3rd November. When we opened the bedroom's wooden shutters, it took us a moment to notice; we were so accustomed to a frosted wintery outlook from our previous visits. The Fab Four love the white stuff, and it brought out the inner child in us all. We rushed outside, and our little black girl, Lani, had a massive attack of the zoomies. Flurries of glittering snowflakes flew into the air as she whizzed around in jubilant circles.

Within the week, there was 77 cm of snow in the forecast. Mark drove an hour down the valley to the supermarket in Pont St. Martin to stock up, since it looked as though we could be snowed in for a few days. The food shops in our nearest villages, Gressoney la Trinité and Gressoney St. Jean, hold very limited stock. The *alimentari* in Staffal has even less, but what it lacks in choice, it makes up for in price. The difficulty of sourcing fresh comestibles in the mountains had led us to bring along our bread maker. Like the government's stockpile of body bags, we didn't yet have an inkling of what a godsend this would turn out to be.

Overnight, we heard a brace of enormous avalanches. One sounded like Thor transforming from hammer-wielding thunder god to DJ Hammer, eking out a twelve-inch extended club remix from his standard seven-inch thunderclap. The following morning, we saw that tons of snow had plummeted down the face of Telcio, directly opposite our apartment.

We'd never seen an avalanche there before, and it felt too close for comfort. The amount of debris was so immense, it had annihilated footpath No. 7, and straddled the River Lys completely. The snow bridge it formed was so substantial, the huge piste machines used it as a river crossing for the rest of the winter.

In order to exit our accommodation, Mark had to dig out a path through hip-deep snow. The puppies had a ball, and a video of their antics helped me unravel one of my life's great mysteries.

My friend Helen once asked,

"Jackie, do you speak foreign languages with a Lancashire accent?"

"I don't know," I replied. "I can't hear my own accent."

The massive guffaw my answer provoked confirmed she thought I was joking. My accent really is that broad!

When I left Lancashire, an early indication that my speech diverged from cut-glass BBC elocution came when I moved to London. In 'The Smoke', everything I said generated undisguised hilarity, and inevitably invited the witty riposte,

"Eeh by gum. Black puddin'. Wheer's yer whippet? We know where *you're* from!"

"What on *earth* do you mean?" I would reply, bemused, in what I believed was crystalline Queen's English.

Then, when I witnessed myself on film during a

role play training exercise at work, the walls of dignified diction came crashing down.

As a wildly gesticulating caricature of a barmaid from the north-of-England TV soap opera, *Coronation Street*, came on screen, I remember thinking, *Who is that woman? I don't recognise her...*

Suddenly, the icy grip of realisation dawned. *Oh my God – it's me...*

I vowed I would never again open my mouth in public.

After a quarter of a century in the south of England, my accent has now softened sufficiently for those in my hometown to level the accusation of,

"Eeh, don't you talk posh these days?!"

Yet Southerners still greet me with, "Eeh by gum. Black puddin'. Wheer's yer whippet?"

I have a talent for mimicry, so, despite my response to Helen, I harboured a smug self-assurance about the authenticity of my foreign diction. Secretly, I believed I spoke French as mellifluously as Coco Chanel. As for Italian, I was certain my delivery was so crisp and clipped, I could pass for a Neapolitan native.

The video of Luisa's dog Lampo playing rather roughly with Rosie in the snow shed light on this, along with another language-based mystery. Why do English-speaking Europeans always reply to my fluent and faultless linguistic efforts in my native tongue?

How do they know? I would ask myself.

When the camera's microphone captured my cries of, "*Lampo! Dolce!*" – Lampo! Gentle! as "Lam-poooah!

Dol-chaay!" it rather deflated my accentual fantasy. Luisa snapped out the entire phrase in almost two syllables, with the 'o' in Lampo as hard as the 'o' in box, and the 'e' in dolce as brief as the one in 'yet'.

So, there you have it. A short video of powder hounds playing proved beyond doubt that I enunciate every foreign language in full "Eeh by gum. Black puddin'. Wheer's yer whippet?" Lancastrian glory!

Meanwhile, metres of snow continued to fall. Stuck indoors, we kept ourselves occupied with home entertainment. The home in question was back in Blighty, where, in our absence, someone had kept the home fires burning.

We fund our travels by renting out property. In one apartment, a fuse box in the bin store underneath the building arced and started a fire. Fortunately, the blaze was contained, but soot and smoke found its way into our flat through the floorboards and skirting. Our tenants were away and nobody was hurt, but we had to move them out to repair the damage – a fun-filled challenge from 1,000 miles away, in the mountains of Italy.

Besides losing all our rental income, we had to pay for our tenants' alternative accommodation. After we'd re-decorated and replaced the carpets in the colours of their choosing, they dragged their heels about moving back. I suppose it's every tenant's wet dream to have their landlord paying their rent!

We had insurance, but of course we didn't receive a full refund. The entire building could have gone up, so we counted our blessings. When the fire brigade identified asbestos within the walls of the bin store, we were still thankful. Once we knew it was there, we had to foot the bill for a specialist to remove it, but at least it had stopped the flames from spreading.

Before you give us a hard time for being irresponsible, slum landlords, a neighbour's electrical arrangement caused the conflagration. When we first moved in, we invested a four-figure sum to make our own electrics safe. The wiring was so bad it took a team of two electricians two days to rectify. To be super responsible, and because you can never have a big enough piece of paper to cover your backside, we also got an electrical safety certificate. Then, it was not a legal requirement for letting, although rightly, it is now – and it probably didn't go amiss in our insurance claim.

The nuts and volts who converted the house into flats did such a shoddy job that, besides being ultimately responsible for the fire, their handiwork nearly vaporised the electrician we employed to put it right. They had not earthed our electrical system, so when our sparky severed a wire to a redundant spur they should have disabled, he discovered a full complement of killer watts running through it. When it exploded, I can honestly say I have never witnessed anyone turn a whiter shade of pale. Had I looked in the mirror, though, I would have seen a matching set, since I was in the room with him. We both nearly choked in a whiteout of acrid gas.

Speaking of whiteouts, back in Monte Rosa, the blizzards kept coming. Heavy snow followed heavy snow, and the forecast predicted more heavy snow to come. This meant the hills were alive with the sound of blasting. The *pisteurs* got busy and deployed explosives from a helicopter to set off avalanches. While our pups quaked in terror at the explosions, it reduced the risk of burial when the resort opened. With so much more snow than the previous year, it looked as though our fat-boy powder skis would get plenty of use.

At the beginning of December, Mark and I enjoyed our first day on the slopes. For skiers, powder snow is Nirvana, Valhalla, and Wonderland combined, with a garnish of Eden, Elysium and Shangri-La. There is no sensation more rapturous and carefree than floating down the piste through knee deep powder snow, inhaling fresh mountain air, with the sun on your back and bluebird skies above.

When our friends Caroline and Graham joined us in Gressoney St. Jean, with their dog Oscar, we were all fully in agreement.

It was shaping up to be a great season.

12. FRIDAY THE THIRTEENTH

"The trouble with practical jokes is that very often, they get elected." Will Rogers

In St. Lucia for my 40th birthday, a local told us, "I wish the French had kept St. Lucia, rather than the English."

When I asked why, he told me,

"Residents of French Caribbean islands all have full French passports, so they can travel wherever they want. British Overseas Territories like St. Lucia don't grant British passports. To go almost anywhere, I need a visa from Barbados."

Effectively, this barred him from leaving the island. St. Lucia was poor, with 30% unemployment. Few St. Lucians could afford travel; reaching Barbados to get a visa was a pipe dream.

He could not choose where to live and work, nor

could he go elsewhere for a holiday, to study or better himself.

For those of us with options, he lived in paradise, yet to him, without freedom of movement, home was nothing more than a beautiful prison.

I felt humbled. By an accident of birth, I had inadvertently won a global lottery. As a British citizen, I held one of the most powerful passports in the world. This encounter made me realise I took my freedom to travel so much for granted that until that moment, I had never even given it a thought.

Now, I'm going to tell you a very British horror story. I must apologise for bringing politics to the party, especially something so toxic and divisive as Brexit, but what happened on Friday 13th is a critical backdrop to decisions Mark and I made about our travelling future. It is integral to our tale, so here goes:

Once upon a time, a little boy proclaimed he wanted to be King of the World.[1]

His name was Alexander Boris de Pfeffel Johnson. He was the great-grandson of Ali Kemal, a prominent Turkish journalist and politician, who sought asylum in Britain in 1909. During the First World War, Ottoman Turkey sided with Germany. To guard against any anti-Turkish sentiment, the little boy's Anglo-Swiss great-grandmother changed her English-born grandchildren's surnames from Kemal to Johnson, her maiden name.

Eton and Oxford educated Alexander Boris de

Pfeffel went on to become one of Fleet Street's highest-paid journalists. His comic talent and elective relationship with the truth[2] reputedly netted him a cool £quarter-of-a mill per ann. For decades, he kept up a steady flow of paint-by-numbers slights against the European Union, where his father Stanley used to work. They were scurrilous and untrue, but entertaining. For example, he claimed EU regulations meant condoms for Italy were smaller, kippers needed ice pillows, and that the EU banned bendy bananas.[3] It sold plenty of papers – and gave him the publicity and accolade he craved. Although twice, his lies were blatant enough to net him the sack.[4]

A dodgy career in journalism was an obvious qualification for a move into politics; first as Mayor of London, then as Foreign Secretary. Eventually, it turned out The Lyin' King's popularity with the public and flexibility with truth was just what the Conservative Party needed to solve a long-running internal schism over Britain's membership of the European Union.

The Johnson was not strongly for or against Brexit. Before declaring his allegiance to Vote Leave, he famously wrote two newspaper articles; one outlining the positives of remaining a member, the other the arguments for leaving.[5]

Brexit has substantial disguised benefits for the privileged few; for example, dodging EU legislation to force the declaration of offshore assets for tax.[6] A camp into which Alexander Boris de Pfeffel and his chums fall neatly. However, the pivotal decision around 'Leave' or 'Remain' appeared to be, 'What's best for Boris?' rather than 'What's Best for Blighty?'

With the keys to Number 10 in his pocket, he clearly backed the right horse, and Britain welcomed in Prime Minister Kemal. Sorry – Johnson.

He scrawled his biggest lie of all down the side of the Brexit bus. He claimed leaving the EU would divert £350 million per week into Britain's NHS (National Health Service.)[7] His Vote Leave campaign also ran an ad claiming 'Turkey, population 76 million, is joining the EU. Vote Leave – Take Back Control'[8]

Imagine that! A load of Turks coming over and nicking our jobs, including the top one!

Following his grand tradition of Britannia Waives the Rules, The Johnson got his house in order before he called a general election to cement his position. To be sure of getting his own way over Brexit, he illegally suspended parliament.[9] When that failed, he expelled all the moderate voices from his party, including Winston Churchill's grandson.[10]

So, on Friday 13th December 2019, the little boy who wanted to be King of the World swept into Downing Street with an eighty-seat majority, and an unassailable mandate to do whatever he wanted, unopposed.

In the UK, truth was in short supply, but irony was alive and well. A massive swing among traditionally left-wing 'red wall' Labour voters brought to power the most right-wing, self-serving government in living memory!

Some people laughed at The Johnson's absurd claims about the EU, but many believed them. He had convinced a slender majority of Britons that turning their back on the world's biggest trading bloc; home to around half of the world's twenty richest countries – right on its doorstep and accounting for 50% of its trade – made great business sense.[11]

It brought to mind *The Great Rock 'n' Roll Swindle*, a mockumentary reputedly about the Sex Pistols in which Malcolm McLaren put together a band who couldn't play, propelled them to stardom, then used them as puppets to cream off the cash and expedite his own agenda.

Aside from any economic arguments, Brexit will weaken Europe. In such uncertain times with dangerous superpowers on the rise, this inevitably poses a risk to the UK. Brexit is our gift to the Kremlin, China, and wannabe nuclear states like Iran. Amid the political kerfuffle, you might not have noticed these three collaborating happily on military manoeuvres.[12]

I am not 100% for or against Brexit. Any course of action involves gains and losses. Like all large organisations, the EU has many faults. However, no one can deny it has presided over an unprecedented period of peace and prosperity in a previously war-torn region of the world.

On the morning of Friday 13th, we awoke to something more terrifying than finding ourselves in a holiday camp haunted by a ghostly slasher called Jason, in the midst of a nocturnal power-outage.

A chain of events that started on Halloween and progressed through Carrie (Johnson's fiancé) moving in prompted Mark to quip,

"If we change No.10's address to Elm Street, the nightmare is complete."

Pro-remain and pro-second-referendum parties actually won more votes than the Conservatives. Ironically, by the same 52–48 percent majority that prompted Vote Leave to claim a conclusive victory. Yet, Britain's first-past-the-post electoral system put The Johnson firmly in the driving seat.[13] Even though important evidence regarding allegations of Russian interference and the impact of Brexit came to light after the vote in 2016,[14] The Johnson's *Great Mock and Poll Swindle* crushed all hope of the electorate being given any opportunity to re-evaluate its decision to quit the EU.

On Friday 13th, the lies to the right had it. Brexit would go ahead, no ifs, no buts – but what exactly did that mean?

Brexit is not a single entity. It can take many forms, but the lack of foresight and planning finally left those with the most extreme viewpoint in charge. Under a Johnson premiership, there would be no second referendum and little chance of a 'soft' Brexit, which would temper the most damaging consequences of exiting the EU, predicted by the government's own research.[14]

For Mark and me, our rights as British citizens were about to change forever.

Ending freedom of movement was a flagship Brexit policy, sold as 'taking back control' of UK borders. The unfortunate side effect is that it also applies to British nationals entering the EU. British citizens without a special visa would be limited to spending only 90 days in a rolling 180-day period in the whole of the Schengen visa-free area. Schengen comprises 26 EU and Non-EU countries, but is expanding with the likes of Romania, Croatia and Bulgaria committed to join.

Brexit spells the end of the year-long motorhome tour of Europe, and stops snowbirds heading south for a warmer winter in Spain. For snomads like Mark and myself, half a ski season in Italy would bar us from even driving through Europe to go elsewhere. Besides, many rest-of-the-world visa agreements are with the EU and Schengen, not the UK, which hinders travel to other countries. And who knew what would happen to passports for dogs?

We needed a solution.

When the news broke on Friday the Thirteenth, I uttered something to Mark that would change our lives for ever.

"I've had enough of Britain. Let's go to Mongolia."

Mongolia is a country three times the size of France, with only three paved roads. Although Big Blue and Kismet had been reliable and well-behaved in conducting us across the Carpathian Mountains and the odd cornfield in Romania, traversing the Gobi Desert could be a step too far.

My Brexit-busting plan needed a lot of research into travel beyond the EU. There were the dogs and visas to consider. Oh, and we would need an overland truck...

In the 2016 referendum, the Conservatives had reduced the most complicated divorce settlement in history to a simple in/out decision. Since they expected 'in' to win, they hadn't bothered with a strategy for maintenance payments or visiting rights should 'out' gain custody.

On the 1st January 2020, Britain left the EU.

After nearly a half century of marriage and three years of wrangling since the decision to separate was made, the UK and EU agreed that nothing would change for a year. During this 'transition period', they would continue to live in the same house while they fought tooth and nail over who got what, with Britain competing to post the finest #LivingMyBestLife, #BetterOffSingle and #AlreadySignedATradeDealWithLichtenstein pictures on her social media feed.

Exactly a month after that ominous Friday the Thirteenth, on 13th January 2020, Mark and I had purchased a 24.5-tonne 1990 Volvo N10 lorry. If you want to know why we named her The Beast. Well. It's because she is!

With a bull nose, 6 x 4-wheel drive and alleged capability of being driven on the moon (if the moon had enough atmosphere to support combustion), The

Beast is a true product of the European Union. Built in Sweden, she spent her working life in the Belgian army. We bought her from a dealer in Holland, renewed Mark's LGV (lorry) licence in Italy, and sourced Austrian trade plates with insurance to transport her back to Britain to convert into our new home.

Mark assured me that taking ownership on the 13th was not a bad sign, but I had one big problem.

"We can't toast The Beast with Limoncello!"

Our drinks cabinet was depleted by the passage of long winter nights. Luckily, a rifle through its darkest corners uncovered a dribble of Dalwhinnie malt whiskey, so we gave her a suitably full-blooded Scottish salutation with hard liquor; *slaintè*.

Thankfully, the transition period meant importing The Beast into the UK did not attract extra paperwork, duty, and a double dose of VAT. From 1st January 2021, imports and exports would cease to be so straightforward.

John Steinbeck was all too prophetic when he said that to destroy a nation, give it too much, and you would soon bring it to its knees; miserable, greedy, and sick.

TV has superseded religion as the opium of the people. As the nation focuses on the issues that really matter – like what happens in the soaps, the Premier League, or who won the *Strictly* dance off, the rich and powerful act in their own interests. A small group of millionaires and billionaires quietly erode our rights in order to use us, and sacrifice our future and that of our planet to line their own pockets. And for what?

To accumulate more stuff they don't need.

Unfortunately, I can't help thinking that as UK citizens, we have taken democracy and our incredible privileges so much for granted that we have been manipulated into giving them away blindly.

Without so much as a second thought.

13. TAKING TOMORROW FOR GRANTED

Carpe Diem – Seize the Day, because you never know what's around the corner...

It is so easy to take tomorrow for granted.

The election result of Friday the Thirteenth brought this into sharp focus. Suddenly, our days of unlimited travel in Europe were numbered.

The realisation that tomorrow is not guaranteed is the very reason Mark and I gave up work to follow our dreams. If there are things you have always wanted to do, you need to seize the day and do them, because you never know what is around the corner.

As I mentioned previously, this had confronted us in spectacular style only the previous year when Mark's mum and brother were both rushed into hospital. While it was considerate of them to co-ordinate their care needs into a single time period, it curtailed both our winter and summer travel plans that year. Yet, the most shocking part was that Nigel was a fit, clean-living guy, who received a shocking diagnosis right out of the blue. A crumb of solace for Mark was that the leukaemia was not hereditary, but it underlined the random nature of how life-changing events can strike with impunity at a moment's notice.

When family ties drew us home to care for those closest to us, we could not have known we were forfeiting our penultimate year of freedom of movement in Europe. Mark's bruv was lucky and made a full recovery from his 'incurable' leukaemia – but not everyone can be assured of receiving such a miraculous second chance.

Nevertheless, even such a blunt lesson so close to home doesn't necessarily stop you from taking tomorrow for granted.

During our working lives, with only a few precious weeks of holiday to sate our voracious skiing appetites, Mark and I were on the slopes at first light and came back only when the lifts closed. Now, with a full ski season to choose from, we had become picky. If we were tired, or the weather was not perfect, we might give it a miss. We took weekends off because the slopes were busy and – horror of horrors – we might have to queue for a lift. I was keen to finish writing my book, *Pups on Piste* and publish it before the ski season ended, so I took a day off here and there as authoring inspiration hit.

Then, even those who are living the dream have work to do. Shopping involved a two-hour jaunt to the supermarket in Pont St. Martin, at the bottom of the mountain. We also visited the vet there and tried to get Italian pet passports for The Pawsome Foursome. Due to notorious Italian bureaucracy, the vet advised against it. However, we got rabies blood titre tests, which cost a fraction of the price we would have paid in the UK. If Britain became an unlisted country in the event of a no-deal Brexit, which we still couldn't rule out, these certificates would help circumvent some potential pet travel fallout. In the UK, Graham and Caroline had shelled out £250 to have Oscar titre tested 'just in case'; we paid €100 for four.

There was a lot of research to do regarding this truck we had bought unseen off the internet. Mark was glued to the mighty Haynes *Build Your Own Overland Camper* manual. A multitude of spreadsheets had sprung into existence; budgets, lists of components, and a myriad of designs for the interior layout. As a couple, we are nothing if not romantic. In bed, we initiated lengthy discussions on solar power systems, the mysteries of lithium vs AGM batteries, and antibacterial water filtration systems. There was also the small matter of Mark's LGV licence, which had lapsed in September, because only four months previously, we decided, "We won't be needing that..."

Now we needed it urgently because on 13th January, exactly a month after The Johnson swept into power on the back of his promise to curtail our freedoms, we were the proud owners of a 24-tonne truck residing in Rotterdam, and needed to drive it home to Bournemouth.

Since the UK was still in its transition period and had not yet left the EU, Mark was able to get the medical and eye test required to renew his licence without flying back to Blighty. Friends posted the forms out to us.

Like every visit to the vet, Mark's appointments were conducted in Italian. This added a layer of multi-lingual mystification, although at the doctor's, Mark's bacon was saved by a chivalrous French Canadian with an Italian wife. Before you could whisper 'patient confidentiality,' he had joined the consultation to translate.

Afterwards, Mark said,

"Doctors are different in Italy. This one looked like a tramp. His clothes were filthy and he had cigarette burns all down the front of his shirt!"

Later, Caroline confirmed this was the same doctor who sang opera to her the previous season; to calm her as he removed a splinter from under her nail.

Then we had guests. Four groups of non-skiing friends came to stay for a week each. We had a lovely time, walking in the snow and visiting mountain huts. Missing an entire month of ski time didn't worry us. After all, there was always tomorrow.

By mid-February, after four months in one place, we had developed a bit of cabin fever.

Mark said, "We can head off in March, after our last guests have gone home. Once we've got the truck back to Britain to convert, we can leave any time. It's a long trip around the Baltics, so the more time we can give it, the better."

We were both excited and eager to get back on the road.

Yet amid a steady stream of guests and the Brexit-fuelled political turmoil, we had largely missed the pathological tsunami brewing on the other side of the world. During a conversation with Matt, a chap from Leatherhead who was renovating a beautiful old stone property on the edge of the village, we joked about reports of a 'zombie flesh eating virus' that had come to light in Wuhan, China.

We'd heard a few snippets in the news, but didn't take it too seriously. I recalled the dire prognostications of a global Armageddon predicted by the British tabloid press around bird flu and swine flu; all of which had amounted to nothing.

"And we were all going to die of Ebola!" I quipped.

Little did we realise that our final, rather abnormal weekend of normality was about to usher in a very abnormal new normal.

14. THE BATTLE OF THE ORANGES – THE CARNEVALE DI IVREA

Fun with the phantom fruit flingers!

Orange is the national colour of the Netherlands. Since Monique and Casper, non-skiing Dutch friends, were staying with us, it seemed only fitting to take them to an Orange Festival.

There are many food fight festivals around the world, based on a variety of cultural, historic or religious traditions. Examples involve throwing flour, wine (decanted), custard pies, and meringues. In food flinging terms, oranges are not the only fruit. The famous Spanish festival *La Tomatina* in Buñol involves tossing tomatoes. (A tomato is technically a fruit!) While all are messy to a degree, the big standout difference with Italy's Battle of the Oranges is that the comestibles mentioned previously all have soft and forgiving properties on impact.

Oranges are far heavier than tomatoes, and come

packaged in thick leathery skin. They are nature's version of a cricket ball. As a projectile, they pack a proper fruit punch! Not only that, the Carnevale takes place in February and the oranges are stored in crates outside. Oranges contain around 80% water, so it's not unknown for the oranges to freeze. At least I have it on good authority (from Caroline, who heard it from a bloke in the pub) that deliberately freezing your ammo to turn it into an icy cannonball was officially banned a few years ago!

Then, never mind the airborne icebergs, there is the matter of duration. At *La Tomatina*, the two sides splatter each other with tomatoes for about an hour. Ivrea's Battle of the Oranges lasts for three pain-filled, produce-pounding days.

Estimates vary, but during the festival, perhaps five-hundred tonnes of oranges are thrown – and when we saw the kids stocking up, they were selective. Only the smallest, hardest fruits went into their ammo bags. Those that could squeeze out supreme agony.

While *La Tomatina* is very well-known and has been described as, 'dangerous, hardcore and about as much fun as you can have with fruit', an Ivrea local told us,

"The tomato festival? That's for boys. The orange festival is for MEN!"

We decided that a city filled with crowds and flying fruit was no place for our pups, so we left Mark in charge of The Fab Four and Oscar, Caroline and Graham's dog. Rather than try to park near a busy festival, Graham drove us all down the mountain to Pont St. Martin where we took the train. From the station in Ivrea, we were not sure where to go, so we followed the crowds and a chap with 'Dave' emblazoned on the back of his shirt.

We lost Dave as we stopped to buy our red hats. These are an essential accessory for festival goers. For €5, sporting a *berretto frigio* (A Phrygian cap), is a precaution which shows your status as a non-combatant to the *aranceri* – the Orange Throwers. However, even though it is an ancient symbol of freedom and liberty, your *berretto* won't grant total immunity from getting juiced or caught in citrus crossfire.

Adorned with our *beretti*, we quickly rejoined Dave and his mates. They hadn't got past the first bar.

The origins of Ivrea's festival date back to the 12th century and the practice of *Droit du Seigneur* – The Lord's Right, which was to have first dibs on bedding the brides of his vassals on their wedding nights. Violetta, The Miller's Daughter – *la vezzosa mugnaia* – was having none of this. The local dignitary, possibly the Marquis of Montferrato, was a tyrant who starved and mistreated his people. In a gesture worthy of *Game of Thrones*, Violetta resisted his rapey advances rather effectively by decapitating him. When she held his severed head above the battlements, she started a people's revolt and, unwittingly, the world's most ferocious fruit-flinging festival.

In the Battle of the Oranges, mask-wearing ruffians

aboard horse-drawn carts represent the tyrant's hench-
men. They progress through the narrow, cobbled
streets and return the orange fire of the nine tribes of
revolutionaries, who await them in the squares around
the city.

The tribes associate with various districts and each
sport their own different colours and costumes:

- Main Town Square
  - *Asso di Picche* (Ace of Spades)
  - *Aranceri della Morte* (Orange Throwers of Death)
- Piazza Ottinetti
  - *Aranceri degli Scacchi* (Orange Throwers of Chess)
  - *Scorpioni d'Arduino* (Arduino's Scorpions)
- Piazza del Rondolino
  - *Pantera Nera* (Black Panther)
  - *Diavoli* (Devils)
  - *Mercenari* (Mercenaries)
- Piazza Freguglia
  - *Aranceri Credendari* (The Credendari Orange
Throwers – honestly, that's how it translates!)
- *Tuchini del Borghetto* (Revolutionaries of the
Borough) is the only tribe whose territory lies on the
far side of the Ponte Vecchio bridge.

Dave sported the *Asso di Picche* colours and his
mates each had the Ace of Spades shaved into the hair
on the back of their heads. We caught up with Dave
periodically as he fortified himself at various bars,
then found ourselves behind him in the queue
for *porchetta* – Italy's wonderful spit-roasted pork,
marinaded in herbs. A *panino porchetta* cost €5, while

€6 got you a *panino* plus a classy plastic tumbler of wine dispensed from a box. While it was not the finest wine, the €6 option was a great choice, since we discovered that lunch already involved queuing twice. Firstly, to purchase a *biglietto* – a ticket to show you had paid and received your wine; secondly for your *panino*. Queueing twice for drinks as well would have made lunch an even more lengthy affair. The Italians are renowned for inventing the 'Slow Food' movement, although I thought it was more about a return to simplicity and wholesomeness as an antidote to consumerism, not queuing!

Duly refuelled, we inspected the ammunition stores in the squares as we passed. Although we wondered whether the huge stacks of wooden orange boxes were armaments for the entire festival, we saw later that there were many equally enormous stacks positioned around the town. Each was carefully labelled for a particular tribe, and for just one of the three days. There were a lot of oranges!

Why throw oranges – who knows? Oranges don't grow in the Alps or anywhere near Ivrea. They ship the inedible, orangey munitions in from Sicily. Some speculate that using oranges might be rooted in chivalric metaphor, since maidens once cast exotic fruit from their balconies to courtiers as tokens. Others suggest they could represent the tyrant's testicles – or simply stones or other ordinance you might deign to discharge in the direction of a deplorable despot.

The weirdness of the tradition suits Ivrea, since the

town itself is a conundrum. On the banks of the Dora Baltea river, the Celts founded it in 500 BC. Some think *Eporedia,* its Celtic name, is derived from *epo* meaning horse (from the Greek '*hippo*') and *reda* – cart.

In 100 BC, the legions arrived, Romanised its name, and left behind a nice amphitheatre. There is also a medieval bishop's palace, a 12th-Century cathedral with a Roman sarcophagus in its crypt, and a 14th-Century castle.

However, in 2018, Ivrea gained UNESCO World Heritage status, not for its millennia of history, but as a 20th-Century Industrial City. This was down to the socio-cultural development started by one Mr. Olivetti, of typewriter fame.

Cormac McCarthy wrote around ten novels, including *No Country for Old Men* and *All the Pretty Horses,* on a pale blue Lettera 32 Olivetti typewriter. Bought in 1963 for $50, it apparently made more than $250,000 at auction in 2009. 'King of Horror' Stephen King and playwright Tennessee Williams were also fans, who tapped their way to literary legendhood on Olivetti keyboards.

Previously, our sole experience of visiting Ivrea had been a tour of the decidedly non-UNESCO industrial estate. There, we sourced Italian data SIM cards from the bounteous agglomeration of mobile phone outlets. Their Pay As You Go deals granted us generous and reasonably priced access to the internet and Netflix from our home at 1,800 metres of elevation. So, for Caroline, Graham and I, it made a pleasant change to take in the historic city; to stroll along the river, through the ancient, cobbled streets and nose around the various squares.

As a horse-lover, I stopped frequently to gaze in awe at the magnificent equestrian parades. The colour orange was not the only connection to the Netherlands. Monique and Casper pointed out the majestic black Friesian horses, with their proudly arched necks and lightly feathered fetlocks. I spotted only one Haflinger; 'The Golden Horse of the Alps' with its flaxen mane and tail.

I mentioned Ivrea's Celtic horsey connections earlier. Another of Ivrea's festivals on the feast of St. Savino is one of the most important horse fairs in Italy.

Italians love the sun. On dull days, they abandon the slopes and more than once, we have spotted an Italian side-stepping up a mountain in order to ski the sunny side of a hill. As such, it was no surprise to learn that they moved the feast of St. Savino from the icy, snowy 24th January to the 7th July simply to take advantage of the weather!

St. Savino's saintly remains came to Ivrea 600 years after his death. They arrived with a relative of Arduino of Ivrea, a self-styled King of Italy from 1002 to 1015, who fled back to Ivrea to escape the plague raging through his duchy. He brought along St. Savino to offer protection from the disease. Despite having no Ivrean connections – and being dead for more than half a millennium – St. Savino got to work immediately. He healed a lame man, cleared the city of the plague, and claimed his place as patron saint and protector of Ivrea.

At the town gate, marshals relieved us of a €10 entrance fee and our refillable stainless-steel water bottles. It was Sunday – bizarrely, there was no entry charge on the Monday and Tuesday. After petting a lot of horses and scoping out the best place to observe the citrussy combat, we positioned ourselves carefully behind the netting which protected the porticoes of Piazza Ottinetti, home of *Scacchi* (Team Chess) and the *Scorpioni d'Arduino* (Arduino's Scorpions).

Plenty of processing and flag waving preceded the action, curiously accompanied by the *Marseillaise* – the French national anthem – and Napoleonic battle marches played on flutes. This was a throwback to the nineteenth century French occupation of Italy, and a convenient amalgamation of a few celebrations into a single *carnevale*.

The powerful rat-a-tat-tat of the drums shook my body and stirred my soul. Then, suddenly, a cart drawn by prancing, plumed horses clattered into the square. At 2 p.m. precisely, the orange-throwing began.

I once attended a rugby international at Twickenham and have walked the road to the old Wembley stadium. The festival atmosphere in Ivrea felt just like that. It was raw, tribal and overflowed with the adrenaline of impending battle.

The *aranceri* gave no quarter. There are rules, but as with rugby union, nobody knows what they are. There is a winner at the end of the three days, judged on – I've no idea. The finer points were lost on me as oranges rained through the air like technicolour cannonballs, exploded against bodies and carts (the horses are *strictly* off limits) and filled our nostrils with their crisp, acidic scent.

Although we had sought refuge behind the protective nets, the momentum of a 150-gram flying fruit, discharged in anger, meant that anyone too close to the netting still received the full force of the blow. Stray produce found its way through many gaping holes, while pulp and freshly squeezed orange juice rained down on us. Savvy festival-goers had wrapped their cameras in cling film or plastic bags. I just tried to turn my lens away from the worst of the syrupy salvos.

After what seemed like hours, and several visits to the square from each of the various aggressors in their carts and colourful regalia, we left the battlefield. Although the nets separated us from the frenetic action and outright aggression in the main melee, even we spectators felt battle-wearied from the hours of furious flinging. As we skidded and skated up the narrow streets on a slime of pulped oranges, it was easy to imagine the slippery aftermath of entrails from bloody medieval skirmishes.

A curious, earthy aroma hung in the air: a combination of sweating horses and their poo, combined with a zingy tang of citrus. In the main square, a stray orange glanced off the back of my arm. It smarted, and I knew there would be a bruise. We passed dazed and confused-looking combatants, battered and bloodied, who had become separated from their tribes. For hours, they had been pummelled by barrages of oranges.

As in any campaign, retreat was not straightforward. To peel off successfully, (Sorry!) required strategy. In the narrow street, we were cornered as *I Seguaci di Re Arduino* – The Followers of King Arduino – battled their way past. We sought refuge from the crashing hooves and flying fruit in what I believe was someone's private hallway, although our presence there was not unexpected. The resident had the foresight to prepare the sanctuary by taping cardboard to their stone floor, and had lined the walls with plastic sheeting. When I saw the state of the roads, I thought they were missing a trick. Citric acid in the orange juice had polished the cobbles to a fine sheen. It could have worked wonders on their flagged floor!

We didn't have the heart or stomach to return and rescue our water bottles, held hostage by 'Elf and Safety at a faraway gate. Instead, we queued the statutory twice – for a ticket, then a restorative coffee – before following a swarm of beaten tourists to the train station for our return journey to Pont St. Martin.

When we arrived in Ivrea, the *carnevale* police were all smiles and good-nature – one even posed for a selfie with Monique. By the time we left, the *carabinieri* had all donned surgical masks. The mood had dropped and become sombre as they herded us towards the station. Later, Caroline recalled it feeling strange and a little sinister, but I was tired after channelling my inner William Wallace, and didn't give it too much thought.

After collecting the car back in Pont, we were held up by the town's own carnival parade. Road closures drew us into the pursuit of several dead-ends. From the various policemen posted at each roundabout, we pieced together the story of how to find a passable route to the one-and-only road that led back home up the Gressoney valley.

Roundabout Number One – "Gressoney?" we asked. "Problem," he replied.

Roundabout Number Two – "Gressoney?" we asked. "Via Perloz," came the enigmatic answer.

Roundabout Number Three – "Gressoney?" we asked. "The road is closed for two hours..."

The carnival in Pont was more subdued than the carrot-coloured war-zone we had left in Ivrea, but we were all carnival'd out. Despite Pont's doggie connections, we decided not to stop and join in. So, while we're stuck in traffic there, let me tell you the legend behind Pont's *carnevale*;

St. Martin arrived in Pont on a pilgrimage along the Franciscan Way to find the only bridge across the River Lys destroyed. He made a pact with the Devil, who promised to rebuild the bridge in a single night, in exchange for the soul of the first living being to cross it. Old Nick duly delivered on his super-quick construction contract, but discovered that while avoiding liquidated damages for late delivery, he had been lax in tying up the finer details regarding payment. The following day, St. Martin sent a dog over the bridge, and thus defeated Lucifer.

Residents burn an effigy of Satan beneath the bridge on Shrove Tuesday to celebrate the triumph over forces of evil by contract law. Of all people, Beelzebub should know, 'the devil is in the detail.'

The moral of the story is – be specific when framing your T&Cs, because you can't even trust a saint.

We giggled as we passed a garage and saw a man fill two lemonade bottles with petrol.

"We had our water bottles confiscated in Ivrea, but petrol bombs are clearly fine in Pont!"

As we wound at less-than-walking-pace behind the carnival procession, we eventually saw the man empty the petrol into a car. He had parked it Italian-style; at a rakish angle, partially blocking the road. We forgave him, since he had clearly run out of fuel. Surely, the other cars parked similarly along the narrow road could not all claim the same excuse.

Along the tiny lane to the hamlet of Perloz, we dodged oncoming traffic through a maze of randomly abandoned vehicles. We climbed the vertiginous hairpins at a snail's pace, in the buzzing wake of an *ape* (pronounced 'appy'), one of the three-wheeled mini agricultural trucks so popular in Italy. Their name comes from the sound of their engines, which make a humming noise like an *ape* – a bee. (They named *Vespa* motor scooters after wasps using the same logic.)

From our high vantage, we could see the miserable

queue on the SR44, the main road along the Gressoney valley. Its sweeping curves were blocked by several miles of coaches, motorhomes and cars, full of weekend skiers trying to return to Milan or Turin. The authorities had not posted signs to warn of potential delays, and the official carnival website remained resolutely silent on the subject of a two-hour road closure. The route through Perloz was way too small to accommodate such large vehicles and thankfully, even though this was Italy, nobody had tried.

As we crossed back on to the SR44 near Lilianes, we mused about how we could possibly describe the events of the day to someone who had not experienced it. It was a strange mix of extreme aggression, absurdity and aromatherapy. We felt like we'd been Tangoed.

I got a groan when I ventured that the orangey aftermath on the streets of Ivrea brought to mind a song,

"Is this the real life? Is this just *Fanta*-sea?

The following day, we received the news that unfortunately, St. Savino could not repel modern plagues, such as the one making a sudden and unwelcome guest appearance during Italy's *carnevale* season. In an unprecedented move, the authorities cancelled the next two days of Ivrea's orange festival along with Venice's famous masked carnival and other similar celebrations around the country. All because of SARS-CoV-2; that mysterious novel coronavirus in China we'd heard a bit about in the news.

Some coronaviruses are responsible for causing the

common cold. With all that Vitamin C flying around, I remember thinking that a cold virus shouldn't find an orange festival so a-peeling.

By finishing on another bad orange pun, you can see I was still just taking the pith, but this crazy weekend with dear friends was the prelude to a dystopian nightmare.

We all had a sense of unreality about what we had witnessed in Ivrea; as if it were a mass delusion. As early as the journey home, what we'd experienced was beginning to seem untrue.

But that was nothing compared with what was to come.

15. OUT OF THE FRYING PAN...

What a difference a day makes...

If you want to make the gods laugh, tell them your travel plans. We escaped Brexit – and found ourselves in quarantine.

Once Monique and Casper returned home, Mark boarded a train for Rotterdam to collect our new truck and deliver it to the UK. They say, 'Let the Train Take the Strain', although between cancellations, missed connections and a freezing night in a bus station in Paris, it was more a case of Let the Train Create the Strain.

Since he was back in the UK, Mark had set aside a week to sort the fallout from the apartment fire. It was an opportunity to co-ordinate the remedial work, put in the insurance claim, get our tenants re-settled, and restore our income as soon as possible. As a responsible adult, he followed the guidelines and had no contact with anyone.

Our closest friend had refused to see him anyway, and coming from Northern Italy, albeit an area unaffected by the virus, Mark cancelled all face-to-face appointments, ate his breakfast in his room, and managed all the issues remotely.

Then, alone in our residence in Northern Italy on Sunday 8th March 2020, I awoke to the headline:

'Coronavirus: Northern Italy quarantines sixteen million people.'

Ironically, the term quarantine derives from the Venetian Italian word *quarantena*, which dates back to the 14th century and the Black Death. It referred to the forty-days (*quaranta giorni*) that ships were required to sit at anchor before docking, to prevent the disease spreading from passengers and crew.

By early March, Italy had the largest number of confirmed coronavirus cases outside China. With hospitals filling with COVID-19 (**CO**rona **VI**rus **D**isease, 2019) patients, Giuseppe Conte, the Italian PM, issued an unprecedented decree: he locked down one quarter of his country's population to stop the virus spreading.

On the evening of that same day, March 8th, he extended the measures to close public spaces, such as museums – and all the ski resorts in the Val d'Aosta – with immediate effect. That included Monte Rosa.

I was all alone, in the centre of Europe's first coronavirus hotspot!

That morning, I had received a worried call from Gressoney St. Jean. Caroline and Graham had decided to evacuate immediately, in case the restrictions were extended to Piedmont and our region of Aosta. Perhaps with the singing doctor in mind, Caroline said,

"I want to be somewhere where I understand the healthcare system and the language..."

She kindly asked if I wanted to flee with them.

"Thanks," I said, "but there's no way I could single-handedly pack up the apartment and caravan in a few hours. I'll be better off waiting for Mark."

"I feel terrible leaving you with Mark away!"

"I'll be fine!" I assured her. "I spent weeks up the mountain on my own in a blizzard last year, when Mark first flew back to look after his mum and brother."

"Our neighbours think we're overreacting..."

"I think you're doing the right thing," I said. "I think we've all underestimated this virus..."

Mark frequently mocks me for over-worrying, so when I called him, I was hoping he wouldn't dismiss my pleas as hysteria.

"You better come back to Italy straight away. Milan has locked down and they've closed the ski resort today."

I urged him to consider a flight, rather than chancing another overland debacle with Ivor the Engine and his merry band of bus replacement services, particularly with the added risk of borders closing.

Mark called me back within the hour. I felt the breath leave my body in a tremendous sigh of relief. For once, he had not only listened, but had taken me seriously.

"I'm booked on a flight from Gatwick to Turin at 6:40 a.m. tomorrow. I can get the train from the airport to Pont St. Martin, which will save you a two-hour drive to *Torino*."

When I collected him from Pont at midday on Monday, Mark told me,

"I was on a 200-seater plane with eighteen passengers. I think everyone had an emergency exit seat. It explains why there was no charge for extra legroom!"

In the list of desirable destinations, Turin had dropped off a cliff.

On the way back up the hairpins to Staffal, we agreed that after four months in Monte Rosa, we both had severely itchy feet. We pledged to pack up and leave with the caravan on Thursday 12th to begin our tour of Poland and the Baltics. With the way our luck runs, we had no intention of departing on another Friday 13th. But what a difference a day makes.

On Tuesday morning, 10th March 2020, the headline had changed. Fortuitously re-united, Mark and I read it together over a coffee.

'Coronavirus: Italy extends emergency measures nationwide. The measures will remain in place until 3rd April 2020.'

We had planned to leave, but our time had run out.

Italy was closed, and we were trapped, but by virtue of one day, our little family could sit it out together. Not everyone was so lucky.

PART III

THE CORONAVIRUS CHRONICLES

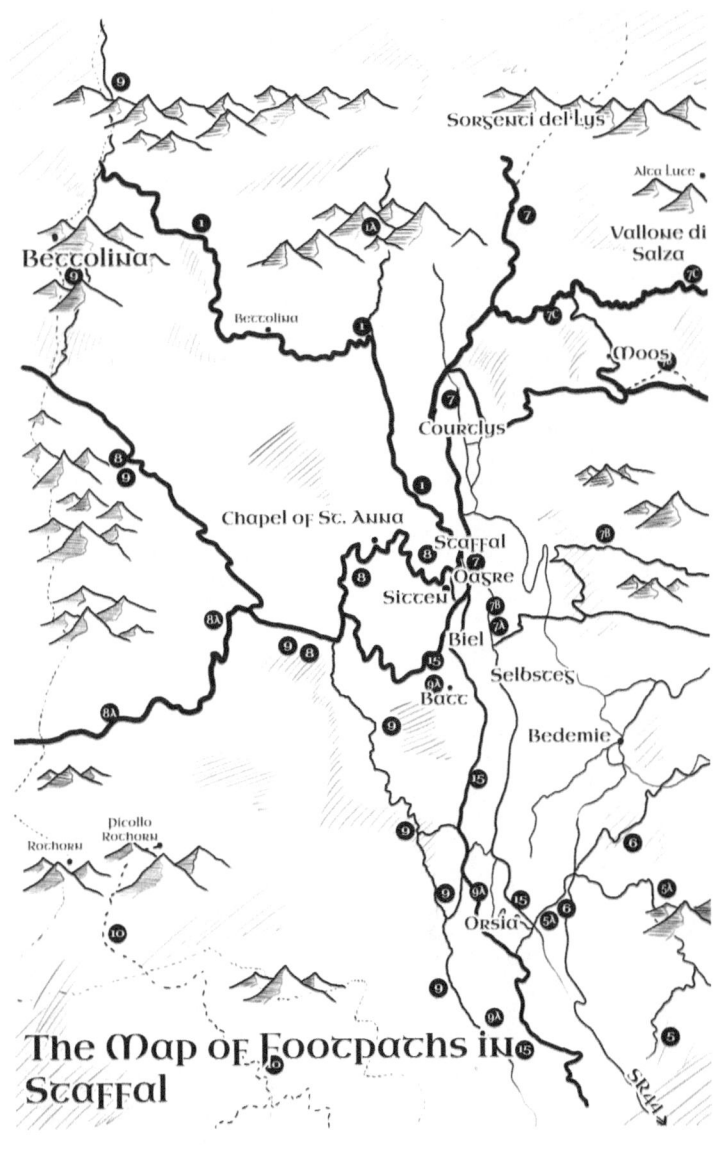

The Map of Footpaths in Staffal

16. LIVING THE DREAM IN LOCKDOWN

Uncertainty becomes the new certainty

On Wednesday, 11th March 2020, the day after the whole of Italy locked down to control the largest coronavirus outbreak outside China, the World Health Organisation (WHO) declared COVID-19 a pandemic; an epidemic that has gone global.

Italy shut her borders and imposed restrictions on all but essential travel. All business and commerce, other than food shops and pharmacies, closed down. Although tourists could go home, their movements had to be justified.

Mark and I had some thinking to do. Just because we could move, did that mean we should?

With hindsight, it might seem strange that our plans to start a tour through Poland and the Baltics didn't go straight out of the window, but coronavirus was a new and developing situation. There were no certainties and we didn't know what to do for the best.

Mark poured scorn on my plan to email the British Consulate to ask, 'Can I leave Italy?'

"It's an emergency, so I just feel we should explore every avenue," I said, but he was right, of course.

Their reply, when it came, was noncommittal. They sent links to their generic travel guidance and signed off with "Please note, all FCO (Foreign and Commonwealth Office) travel advice is published on GOV.UK, there is no additional information our consular officers can provide in response to your enquiry."

Mark crowed over my cataclysmic failure. Patience and understanding were another casualty of coronavirus.

"I told you so!" he said, using more words than were strictly necessary. "Government departments are all about as useful as a chocolate shopping trolley for carrying hot custard."

Clearly, we were on our own. We considered our situation; could we outrun the virus, avoid being locked down, and find somewhere safe to sit out the pandemic? It seemed unlikely. We reasoned that with the virus spreading rapidly, wherever you found yourself, COVID-19 would inevitably be coming soon to a country near you. Moving would not safeguard us from infection or lockdown; in fact, it would probably do the opposite. We recalled that a few short weeks ago in Italy, it was business as usual, and no one was talking about coronavirus. How quickly that had changed – and how quickly it was likely to change elsewhere.

Our apartment was the last building at the end of the Gressoney valley, in a tiny village at 1,800 metres. Our nearest neighbour was Monte Rosa, the second highest peak in the Alps, surrounded by a national park full of snow-silent wilderness.

Piedmont separated our region, the Aosta Valley, from the major coronavirus hotspots in Lombardia and Veneto. In Aosta's 1,200 square miles, there were only eight confirmed COVID-19 cases; the same as in the English county of Hampshire. An upward trend in infections suggested the situation would change for the worse, but we felt safe and comfortable in our apartment. The village was empty. Mark and I accounted for a quarter of Staffal's entire population – and The Fab Four increased it by fifty percent. In the midst of the outbreak, we had found the calm in eye of the storm.

With nobody around, we were not at risk of infection and presented no risk to others.

Announcements on Wednesday 11th March vindicated our leaning towards staying where we were. Denmark became the second European country to lock down. On Thursday 12th, Morocco closed its borders with Spain, which had already locked down four towns to contain the spread of the virus. Four days later, on 16th March, the Health Secretary advised a UK-wide lockdown, which came into force on the 20th.

As Britain closed down, with the timescale for re-opening uncertain, BBC News put out a call for UK nationals to go home. They warned that those who failed to return could be stuck abroad indefinitely.

I mentioned earlier that renting out property funds our travels. Implementation of The UK Coronavirus Act 2020 imposed a ban on evictions. Of course, we didn't want to kick out our tenants. We're not monsters! However, although we were homeowners, that rendered *us* homeless.

A few weeks into lockdown, 'Returning to the area you are normally resident' was no longer a justifiable reason for travel in Italy. Ferries had suspended all passenger services and while Eurotunnel might have been a possibility, all friends and family upon whom we could impose ourselves fell into the 'vulnerable' category. We had the caravan, but throughout the UK and Europe, campsites were closed, and the bungalow whose lawn we'd camped on for the previous summer was sold.

We literally had nowhere to go.

Initially, the thought of spending an indefinite lockdown alone in a national park with the ski slopes to ourselves seemed like a sterling idea. 'Skins' for the bottom of our skis would allow us to walk uphill then ski down. But when news briefings showed Italy's hospitals overflowing, with scenes more akin to what you would see in a war-zone, we changed our minds. It was an era of personal responsibility. The last thing the over-stretched emergency services needed was some numpty injuring themselves skiing – and who knew whether Mountain Rescue would even come and get us if we did. We had to take care. At 1,800 metres in an abandoned Alpine village, help was a long way away.

At first, we just enjoyed the scenery and walked the dogs locally. In our new quest to avoid injury, we refrained from being too adventurous. Yet, falling through snow in our garden, I ended up waist deep in a rock crevice, and Mark got a boot full of water when his foot slipped into an uncovered drain. Usually, we would have laughed heartily at such slapstick misfortunes, but in the circumstances, our reaction was sober relief that neither of us had twisted an ankle or broken a bone.

We ceased using the lift in the apartment block for the same reason. If we became stuck, who knew if or when help might arrive? Although now that we were deprived of skiing, at least the stairs provided some much-needed exercise.

They say trouble comes in threes. Free and unlimited access to healthcare guarantees that nothing will happen, but the day after lockdown, I lost a filling. Ironically, it was liberated by the biodegradable silk dental floss I had reported to Amazon as missing in action. It had finally arrived three months late – from

China. I was suspicious, and almost prodded my parcel into quarantine with a stick. A Google search confirmed that coronavirus can't survive on a cardboard box in a shipping container for a quarter of a year, so it was fine to touch a Chinese package without donning a full isolation suit!

Trouble number two came when Mark opened a jar of peppercorns and a shard of flying plastic hit him in the eye. His eye swelled shut and he had to wear a blindfold for twenty-four hours. Fortunately, there was no lasting damage to his cornea. Then, the following morning, Kai nearly broke his leg. He jumped off a bench with his hind paw caught between the slats.

If they were even open, the nearest medics were all an hour away at the bottom of the mountain. Thankfully, everyone made a full recovery – apart from me. I would just have to live with my lost filling until my freedoms were restored. Then, I could seek out the Italian cousins of the famous Scottish dentist, Phil McCavity.

Now safely home, Caroline and Graham revealed that lockdown in the UK was very different and far less stringent than in Italy. For us, the *carabinieri* patrolled the mean streets of Staffal, even though they were deserted. Staffal's tiny food shop was closed, with the nearest mini market in the next-but-one village of Gressoney St. Jean.

The rules permitted only one person in a car. To buy food, one of us had to fill in a form with our name, address, passport number and reason for travel. We had to present this at the police checkpoint in the next village, Gressoney la Trinité. This controlled all vehicle movements on the single road up and down the valley. To ensure we could get back to the apartment, we had to carry our rental agreement as proof of address.

Since St. Jean's mini market barely stocked a potato, our fortnightly winter routine had been a two hour round trip down the mountain to stock up in the Conad supermarket in Pont St. Martin. During lockdown, St. Jean's mini market closed. Even then, the *carabinieri* at the checkpoint refused to let us through.

"You must order by phone."

Online grocery shopping had not hit our part of the Alps. The *carabinieri* gave us a number to call. Despite diligent daily appointments on the internet with Duolingo's Italian course, our fledgeling conversational skills were not equal to a telephone order of groceries. Impatient operatives fired language at us like a gun.

Italian is a minefield when it comes to mispronunciation. *Pesce* (pronounced 'peshay') means fish, while *pesche* ('peskay') are peaches. Fail to linger long enough on your 'n's and all of a sudden, instead of ordering *penne* ('pen-nay' – pens or tubular pasta) you're ordering *pene* – or penis. Penis with peach sauce? It was not how I wanted to get through lockdown – and I certainly didn't want to suffer murder by mispronunciation.

Like Mark, you might think I'm being melodramatic. An accusation he once levelled at me was,

"You remind me of a German vegetarian. You constantly fear the wurst!"

But I give you Dr. Charles Budd Robinson, a Canadian botanist working in Indonesia, who got into terrible strife over a coconut. Apparently, instead of asking villagers to get a boy to 'chop down a coconut' – *porong kelapa* – he actually asked *potong kepala* – or 'chop off his head.' This seemingly miniscule miscommunication was enough to convince locals that the previously popular Dr. CBR was a head hunter. So, they killed him.[1]

In the end, it was our knowledge of Italy's untouchable daily ritual; *pranzo* (lunch), that saved us from starvation. Between the hours of twelve and two, the checkpoint at Trinité was unmanned because the *carabinieri* went for lunch. Not even a pandemic can pull the plug on *pranzo*. It provided an infallible two-hour window for Mark to nip down to Pont for supplies. If the police apprehended him on the return journey, we still had food.

The checkout staff at the Conad supermarket kindly sorted Mark out with a mandatory face mask for €5. They explained that to maintain social distancing, only one person could occupy each one metre square marked with tape on the shop floor. Mark made our fortnightly forays with a slight sense of guilt, and the risk of a €3,000 fine, but we had to eat.

Our fortunate existence with freedom to roam within the boundaries of our village continued for three weeks. Until the day we met an exceedingly unpleasant chap while out with the dogs on the river.

"You should not be here! Aosta valley is closed!" he snapped at us.

He obviously assumed we were tourists, who had ignored quarantine to come up the valley for a jaunt. We couldn't fathom how he thought we'd got past the checkpoints.

"We live here!" we replied loftily. Then his horrible little dog lunged and bit Lampo, who accompanied The Fab Four on most of our daily *passegiate*.

"I bet he calls the police and dobs us in!" I joked.

Coincidentally, on our way back, the community police patrol accosted us in the vast abandoned car park in the centre of Staffal.

A very nice policewoman wound down her window. She spoke in English, which strengthened our suspicion that Mr. Obnoxious was a squealer.

"The guidelines have changed," the lady officer told us politely. "The new advice is *Io Resto a Casa* – I Stay Home. Now, you may not leave your garden."

"But there's nobody here!" we exclaimed.

She smiled and said, "The rules must apply to everyone."

She was right, of course. In a national emergency, there's no place for individuals to interpret the regulations to suit themselves – even amid a nation of independent-minded rule breakers like Italy.

With sinking hearts, we returned to the apartment and lamented our situation. Freedom to walk in our beautiful surroundings had been the one saving grace of being stuck. Now, we would be confined to barracks.

Our lockdown honeymoon was over.

17. DON'T PANIC!

A Lesson about Viruses from a Mutant Gordon Ramsay

"Thank *God* you've phoned. I was so worried." My poor dad already had us dead and buried.

The British media had lost no time before launching into its usual Doomsday frenzy of hysteria and scaremongering. Not long back from the UK, Mark told me,

"It was chaos. The supermarket shelves were empty. You couldn't get loo rolls for love nor money – and there was *nothing* but coronavirus on the news. There was panic-mongering everywhere. Even on Radio 4!"

Radio 4. Britain's last bastion of sense and impartiality.

I am a worrier, but through thirty years of dabbling with extreme sports, I have learned to adopt a balanced view of risk. My scientific background taught me to ignore hearsay, and appraise only carefully tested facts. It also afforded me insider information about the sensational "mutant virus" headlines plastered all over the front pages. Let me explain.

There is nothing remotely unusual about a mutant virus. All viruses mutate. Viruses do get a bad press because they cause disease, but let's put that unfortunate side-effect to one side for a moment, because the biochemist in me demands that you marvel at these incredible little biological machines!

Viruses are invisible, sub-microscopic packages of genetic material that float around the place. They are not really alive; they are not conscious and cannot reproduce by themselves. Their raison d'être is simply to find a suitable host to help them replicate.

Different viruses can infect every type of cellular organism, whether animal, plant or bacteria. In fact, 'phages (bacteriophages) – viruses which attack bacteria – might one day save the human race. Profligate over-prescribing of antibiotics has created multi-resistant strains of bug. When antibiotics cease to be effective, which is already happening, the deployment of 'phages might be the answer.

Antibiotics kill bacteria. They are totally useless against viruses. If you must have a pill to cure a viral illness, like a cold or flu, you might as well take chocolate buttons. At least chocolate has some therapeutic properties – not against viruses, I'll grant you, although you're losing nothing there. On the up side, chocolate tastes nice, doesn't annihilate all your 'good' bacteria, and doesn't reveal our hand to the 'nasty' ones. Wanton exposure to humanity's full antibiotic arsenal has given prudent pathogens the most impeccable opportunity to mutate and develop resistance to our best line of defence against them.

The virus modus operandi is to invade a living cell, then take it over like a little alien. A bit like sweary television chef Gordon Ramsay taking over someone's kitchen. Once inside, he implements his own menu. To do this, he uses his own biological recipe book – DNA (*Deoxyribo Nucleic Acid)* or RNA (*Ribo Nucleic Acid*) – to turn the kitchen into a virus factory. Then virus Gordon creates millions of identical copies, or clones, of himself.

If Gordon were a respiratory virus, he'd then make his host cough and sneeze to spread disease. This would give all the baby virus Gordons a supersonic send off. Then, unleashed upon humanity, they would each set out on their quest to find a new kitchen to take over.

Sometimes, Gordon's copies of himself are not quite exact; random mistakes with the ingredients change their genetic blueprint in an accidental process known as mutation. This is how new variants of Gordon develop. One imperfect copy might swear too much and get its television contract cancelled for being too toxic. That version of Gordon will die out.

But an improved Gordon – one who can get into kitchens more easily – becomes more transmissible. Natural selection favours the mutant virus Gordon. He will be the one who ends up making the most copies of himself, so he develops into the dominant strain. He might become so successful that he even spreads beyond his own national boundaries. You might suddenly discover him across The Pond, judging *Masterchef*, or making US versions of *Hell's Kitchen* and *Kitchen Nightmares*. Left unchecked, he could take over the world...

Like bacteria, viruses reproduce quickly; one generation can last as little as a few hours, so the genetic makeup of both viruses and bacteria can transform rapidly. Imagine how swiftly virus Gordon would evolve if he could produce millions of grandkids in a matter of days. You might end up with a non-sweary Gordon, who could be screened before the watershed. He would soon land his own educational children's series, star in a Hollywood blockbuster, and become the BBC's news anchor.

This short life cycle is how viruses manage to adapt swiftly enough to leap from one host species to another, and why the flu vaccine has to be tweaked every year to account for new variants.

The good thing is that it is not advantageous for a virus to be too deadly. One reason Ebola didn't go global is that most patients died before they infected anyone. Over time, as host immunity evolves, and the virus perfects itself, it will become endemic, like the common cold. And polite mutant virus Gordon, who will fade from the limelight to continue his laudable charity work in the background, with only an occasional lapse back into profanity making the news.

Although panic and misinformation raged across the internet, Mark and I did not feel in mortal peril. We soon deduced that catching the virus was not an automatic death sentence. Governments put containment measures in place to prevent the rapid spread, protect the sick and vulnerable, and avoid overwhelming hospitals with patients who developed serious complications. The watchword was 'Flattening the Curve'; slowing down the number of people infected at any one time so the healthcare services could cope.

The WHO stated, "Most people who become infected experience mild illness and recover, but it can be more severe for others." Statistics reported by the press showed Italy's typical COVID-19 casualty was 81 years of age, with three serious underlying health conditions.

Mark and I were sanguine about the situation. Isolated up a mountain, catching the disease was not a concern. While we would rather avoid infection, since we were young (ish!) and in good health, we could reasonably expect to make a full recovery.

Yet the virus had the potential to kill some, and lockdown the potential to destroy livelihoods. The statistics revealed a terrifying truth. One in five cases (20%) required hospital treatment, with one in twenty needing critical care. Scale that up and you see 100 cases of COVID-19 demanded 5 ICU (Intensive Care

Unit) beds. Leap to 100,000, and you suddenly need to find 5,000 ICU places.

According to the BBC, the UK's entire ICU capacity was 4,000.

Italy has a similar population to Britain, and one of the best resourced healthcare systems in Europe with nearly double the UK's 4,000 critical care beds. But even in a pandemic, patients still get sick with diseases other than COVID-19, and a highly infectious virus ripping through front-line workers caused dire staff shortages. The numbers made it easy to see how the drama so quickly became a crisis.

Coronavirus in Italy was the perfect storm. A by-product of their exceptional healthcare system is one of the most elderly populations in the world. In addition, Italians are a sociable bunch, and many extended families live together. Coronavirus soon overwhelmed the hospitals, forcing upon doctors the unimaginable horror of deciding who received life-saving treatment, and who they left to die.

Italy's COVID-19 death toll skyrocketed into the tens of thousands.

My grandfather was born in 1900. He lived through two world wars and the 1918 Spanish flu epidemic – without the benefit of Britain's free and universal National Health Service. These days, few in the West have ever faced a truly existential threat. Also, when trying to resolve uncertainty in times of stress, people's ability to judge and evaluate facts reduces. People need to believe, and seek simple answers to complex problems.

Sense and critical thinking did not abound and panic took over. Coronavirus became an infodemic, as some on social media shared all kinds of outlandish theories, 'just in case they are true'. Others claimed it was all a hoax to control people; that the virus didn't exist, or had been engineered in a lab in China or released by Bill Gates. I urged for calm, and asked people to check their facts before sharing. I suggested that, somewhere between licking seats in public toilets in a gesture of defiance, and bathing in bleach while wearing an isolation suit, there was a balance.

In the week that Douglas Adams' cult classic *The Hitchhiker's Guide to the Galaxy* turned 42 (= the answer to life, the universe and everything) it felt eminently suitable to reiterate the words written comfortingly on its cover: Don't Panic!

I even changed them to reflect the situation in the UK and urged, Don't Panic Buy!

Yet, despite his concern for us, my 85-year-old dad refused to let my brother or I to do his shopping online. He said, "I like to do it myself – and I'm only in the supermarket for twenty minutes." Too quick for coronavirus.

Mark's brother, whose immune system was still weakened as he recovered from leukaemia, ignored our pleas to stop taking the ferry and train every week to visit a friend.

Mark's 90-year-old aunt and uncle, who live with their son, dismissed our concerns about him commuting daily on the tube into London, the UK's coronavirus hotspot.

It seemed everyone was panicking – except those who needed to.

18. HOW WE MADE OUR ISOLATION SPLENDID!

Our attempt to view lockdown as a precious gift of time...

Being stuck in isolation placed a strain on many relationships, and ours was no different. One morning, Mark uttered the words that, as a wife, I never wanted to hear,

"I've tidied up the bathroom cabinet."

My heart sank. I wouldn't be able to find anything for months.

With Mark, the process of rearrangement is ceaseless, but definitely worsens when he is at a loose end. It keeps me busy, though. We have few possessions, but I never know where any of them are; especially if I am stupid enough to seek them out where I last put them.

Despite our itchy feet, we applied irritating positivity to our situation and tried to view lockdown as a precious gift of time.

Obviously, searching for my belongings occupied

most daylight hours, although I also found time for tasks I'd forever been meaning to do. I set about transcribing my old travel journals from paper to Microsoft Word, and started to learn Russian.

"Why Russian?" you might ask.

Well, remember that truck we bought when we hatched our Brexit-busting plan to head east? Russian is the world's eighth most spoken language. It facilitates communication in Belarus, Ukraine, The Stans, (*Uzbeki-, Kyrgyz-, Kazakh-, Tajiki- and Turkmeni-*) as well as Armenia, Azerbaijan, Georgia, Moldova, Latvia, Lithuania, Estonia, Israel – and those outposts of the Russian Federation found in annexed territories such as Crimea, and expensive French ski resorts like Chamonix and Courchevel.

Besides being a common second language in much of Eastern Europe, it is also related closely enough to Slavic languages to grant a basic understanding. Apparently, few Russians speak English – and signs in Russia are written in Cyrillic letters. Thus, if I wanted to navigate to St. Petersburg, *and* fulfil my long-held ambition to be a cosmonaut like Yuri Gagarin, Russian was a good option. Plus, I'll quote you a well-known Russian proverb;

'Лучше один раз увидеть, чем сто раз услышать' – It is better to see once than to hear a hundred times.

Very pertinent to travellers – and that big old stream of Cyrillic illustrates just how useful the ability to decipher the Russian alphabet on road signs will be!

When Britain locked down, I got a text from the UK Government, which was nice. It said I could go out once per day for exercise. If only...

Since we were grounded, Mark and I elected to cripple ourselves. We partook of an online fitness class and couldn't move for two days. I worried it was because we were getting old, but Mark assured me the pain was the same whenever we started a new training routine. In every sense, our freedom of movement was scuppered!

A meme was circulating on Facebook; "If landlords get a mortgage holiday, tenants should get a rental holiday. Share if you agree!"

It was the usual simple black-and-white-soundbite-with-lack-of-facts – and no mention of expressions such as, 'ongoing landlords' insurance and maintenance charges'; 'accrual of extra mortgage interest'; or 'massive hike in payments after the so-called 'holiday''.

I'm not going to pretend Father Christmas doesn't exist, that would be ridiculous, but I am going to share with you one of life's shocking truths. Lending institutions are not benevolent charities. They're in business to please the shareholders and enrich their bosses, and they do this by turning a profit. Now, I want you to think of a number – let's say, a few months' extra interest on thousands of buy-to-let mortgages – then multiply it by five, ten, twenty, or however many years the loans still have to run.

I know!

That's a profit lottery I'd like to win too!

Straight away, two of our tenants made the call. One had only just moved in to our recently vacated property. Our agent told us cheerily that they had been 'furloughed'. This unfamiliar word meant the UK Government paid them 80% of their salary to stay away from work. He also said we were the only landlords in his portfolio whose tenants had asked for a rental holiday. Lucky us!

"But their rent is our only source of income," we pleaded. "We have rent and bills to pay too – and there is zero government help for landlords," – a couple more facts that escaped the Facebook meme. "We're having two roofs replaced – and we've just had the fire. We still have all that to pay for!"

It is a popular myth that landlords are all evil millionaires, whose sole aim is to exploit their tenants by charging them top dollar to live in a slum. Our property management philosophy is to provide comfortable, well-maintained accommodation that we'd be happy to live in ourselves. So happy that in fact, we previously did! By doing this for a reasonable price, we attract good tenants who stay longer and look after the place: all of which saves us money and hassle while we're abroad.

We achieved financial independence and retired early through an old-fashioned concept called going without – or 'economising and saving' as it is sometimes known. To keep our living costs down, we spend most of the year in a caravan, while someone else gets the benefit of our property.

Banks. They have lots of money!

Isn't that where folk usually go if they are a bit short? Instantly demanding that a complete stranger, whose property you happen to rent, hands over 100% of their income for an indefinite period as an unsecured loan to bail you out of a financial commitment into which you entered voluntarily, was a new one on me.

But these were extraordinary times. We agreed to a month's grace while their government money came through, although ultimately, our tenants surprised us by doing the decent thing. When we offered to release them from their new tenancy without penalty, as it seemed they couldn't afford it, they solved their financial troubles immediately in a much more traditional way – The Bank of Mum and Dad.

I weathered all this, along with concerns about distant loved ones, but twenty-one days into isolation, seven days into complete confinement in the house, the UK went into lockdown. When the BBC put out its call for UK nationals to return, I had a little wibble...

I knew we were stuck and had nowhere to go, and it got to me.

And, to paraphrase the inimitable words from the film *Airplane*, 'I guess we picked the wrong time to give up antidepressants...'

In the hope it might help break down the taboos and shame surrounding mental health, I have been open about the fact that Mark and I suffer from depression. Initially, we resisted antidepressant medication, but finally accepted its role in our recovery. Pride gave us a strong desire to quit as soon as possible so, in line with best practice, we had reduced our dosages gradually over the previous year.

We had other compelling reasons to stop. Doctors will only prescribe a three-month supply, so getting sufficient medication to cover a long trip abroad was impossible. Cutting down eked out our supplies. However, more pressingly, along with a surprising number of non-prescription drugs, antidepressants are illegal in some countries we planned to visit.

Remember the film, *Midnight Express*? It was based on a true account of a hash-smuggling student's horrific and brutal incarceration in a Turkish prison. Some over-the-counter opioid painkillers, such as codeine, are classed as controlled drugs in many countries, and carrying a *Vicks* inhaler can get you jailed in Japan. Hence, giving up seemed the best strategy to avoid heavy fines, imprisonment or deportation.

Crises bring out the best and the worst in humanity and coronavirus was no exception.

In my communications on social media, I sought to

be objective about the pandemic. I questioned fake news and countered misinformation with facts, but this was not a popular stance. People do love to be caught up in a drama, and nobody is interested in good news. My dispassionate approach attracted online abuse, and one 'friend' generously asserted that I had no business having a wibble about being stranded far from home, since others were worse off.

There is invariably someone worse off, but that is no reason to dismiss anyone's feelings, anxieties, or concerns as inconsequential. It all felt very real to me. Besides, using that logic, only one person in the entire world can justifiably feel down.

In the end, I self-isolated from Facebook.

For me, one weird symptom of depression is an aversion to speaking on the phone. I can just about manage a five-minute conversation with my dad every week, but detained indefinitely in an abandoned village, 1,000 miles from home, Facebook was my principal social contact with the outside world.

Fortunately, I am lucky to have some genuine friends. Amid the noise and bluster, I received a few supportive and understanding messages, so I eventually re-connected with social media, but in a limited way. Immediately, I blocked all the negative contacts and communicated directly only with those who enriched my life. I ceased doom-scrolling through the depressing news feed in the vain hope that it might reveal a precious nugget of new information that would somehow help to make sense of it all.

I posted nothing controversial, declined to comment on misinformation, and deleted negative comments. Amazingly, some individuals still hijacked my upbeat posts with doom and gloom. They were promptly expunged from my friends list.

Part of the stress of the pandemic was the unsettling sense that everything was beyond my control. It felt good to regain some mastery.

So, my descent into the indulgent abyss of Self Pity was mercifully short. I emerged cheerful once again, with renewed perspective; grateful that my situation was not worse. Despite being housebound in a deserted village, we had everything we needed and zero coronavirus cases in the wider community. We were as safe there as anywhere and on a day-to-day basis, we were happy enough. If the circumstances were different, we might have really enjoyed it. What irked us was the nagging knowledge that we couldn't leave.

The real blessing was that The Fab Four had no idea what was going on in the world. Every day was normal, except we didn't walk as far as usual. A visit to the bin store, slightly outside the premises, was now an adventure. Sometimes, Mark and I held back the recycling, so we could make an extra trip. In the confines of the garden, the pooches would happily play ball, chase, or dig for marmots.

Inside, having a puppy to cuddle was the best therapy.

And failing that, there was always wine!

19. THE ITALIAN JOBSWORTH – A BRUSH WITH THE LAW IN CORONAVIRUS LOCKDOWN

We come to terms with bureaucracy at its most bizarre

A recurring feature of our lockdown in Monte Rosa was my Morning Worries.

As we sipped coffee in bed, admiring the snowy peaks through huge picture windows, my night fears would bubble to the surface. When they frothed over and I was compelled to blurt them out, my beloved addressed each individually, with characteristic tenderness and empathy.

"What if an eagle carries away the dogs when we go to Mongolia? Or what about the legendary Monte Rosa vulture and the wolves, whose very existence we have only just discovered?"

He laughed out loud at that, but showed sufficient concern to check out and relay Alaska Fish and Wildlife's assertion that, *"Eagles Don't Eat Children or Pets"*[1] – and that wolves and wild dogs respect a pack.

His unwarranted response to my Morning Worry about genuine winter hazards was,

"Yes. I'll be careful not to be speared by a falling icicle, because when they discover my body next to a pool of water, only lateral thinkers will be able to work out what happened."

A recurring theme amid my Morning Worries was the pressure of snow on Caravan Kismet's roof, and the peril posed by polar temperatures to the longevity of her leisure battery.

"The manufacturer's adverts show a bloke *and* a car perched on top of the caravan!" was Mark's response to the weight issue.

"But the car was not resting on the solar panel, aerial and roof lights!" I pleaded.

I have read horror stories about owners approaching their recreational vehicles in the spring, only to find the electrics all dead and batteries smothered in a corrosive acidic crust. Denied life-giving energy from snowed-up solar panels, and with a trickle charge from the mains out of the question, Mark irascibly agreed to disconnect Kismet's battery as a dual protection – to mitigate against months of sub-zero temperatures *and* wifely harassment.

However, when the climate at 1,800 metres achieved a snow-softening 18°C, which cleared Kismet's roof and solar array, we decided to re-connect her battery. Well, I decided, and relayed my wishes to Mark. He agreed immediately, in the interests of an unruffled morning coffee.

Who knew what a Pandora's box this would become, when we were caught by the law in possession of a caravan!

We had parked Kismet in the centre of the village all winter. Well, almost all. As loosely arranged the previous year with The Hotel Manager, she was originally in the hotel car park next door to our residence. Then, one lunchtime, The Manager issued an eviction notice. He told Mark she had to be gone that afternoon.

"But she's got one wheel removed for security and is buried up to her windows in snow," Mark pleaded.

"I'll give you a shovel," he replied.

Mark brought his frustration back to the apartment reception, where Luisa was filling the dogs with biscuits.

"*Lui è arrabiata!* – He is angry!" Luisa deduced as she observed Mark's face and neck throbbing with the beetroot hue of a bubbling cauldron of *borscht.* He railed against the stupidity.

"*Perché oggi?*" – Why today? The hotel was not even open. "*Perché non domani o il giorno dopo?*" – Why not tomorrow or the next day?

Luisa called The Manager and put to him that very point.

The French have the word '*Non*' and the Gallic Shrug with which to convey firm Frankish mulishness. "*Imposs-eee-bile*" is the classic intonement of Italian intransigence, and that is exactly what came back.

Tomorrow or the next day was simply not an option. *Oggi* was obligatory.

The Manager had suffered a sudden bout of amnesia about his vague agreement to host Kismet for the winter in a quiet corner of his car park. His memory didn't improve even when we offered to bung him €100. He remained deaf to our pleas.

"She's seven metres long. Where can we put her?"

He closed the conversation with, "Not my problem."

Dear Luisa came to our rescue and told us we could place Kismet in the village, "*Oltre la fontana*" – Past the fountain.

Now, we were well into our sixth visit and fourth full season in the tiny hamlet of Staffal. I was adamant that the gods had never revealed to me a fountain. My mistake was to imagine something like the perpendicular water cannon in the stately grounds of Chatsworth House, which propels spray high into the stratosphere. Luisa walked me down to the end of the road and showed me the fountain – an animal trough in a roughly hewn structure that I had always assumed was a rustic bus shelter. I guess it was a drinking 'fountain', or maybe the whole water feature thing was simply lost in translation, like Dr. C.B. Robinson's coconuts.

The mere thought of moving Kismet whipped up a maelstrom of Morning Worries. Digging her out of three feet of snow took up the entire afternoon, although The Manager got someone to clear the rest of the car park with a machine. We were not about to move her in the dark, so Mr. Manager had to put up with his unwanted guest for an extra night. I could not sleep; I foresaw finding her the following dawn, battered to a pulp by a sledgehammer wielding Hotel Manager. In my mind, The Manager had taken on the wild-eyed persona of Jack Nicholson in *The Shining*, the film Mark forced me to watch for the first time in my life while we were snowed in at our spookily deserted apartment block.

I am not a fan of the genre 'Horror' and had to be escorted on nocturnal comfort breaks for several months after seeing *The Sixth Sense*. You can imagine the effect on me of a movie like *The Shining* when I was basically trapped inside the set!

But imaginary caravan crushing was as nothing to the genuine fear of towing our pride and joy down the icy slope from the car park onto the road. I envisaged scenes of untold carnage; Kismet jackknifing then skidding forwards to overtake Big Blue; overturning on the corner and landing, along with my soul mate and our dreams, in the inescapable, watery clutches of the ice-bound River Lys...

Mark dismissed my fears with a casual, "It will be fine."

In reality, my Moving Day Worries were unfounded. Mostly.

Mark negotiated the icy slope without incident, although another *arabbiata* moment developed while reversing Kismet up a slight incline into her final resting place beyond the 'fountain'. I maintained a diplomatic silence to Mark's Krakatoan outburst on the subject of snow chains,

"I'm not putting the freakin' snow chains on to get over that one, small patch of black ice!"

With repeated approach attempts, Big Blue's skidding drive wheels had soon polished the unavoidable icy square to a frictionless sheen, upon which it was impossible to gain traction. I kept my counsel, but knew the Fates had conspired to lead us towards the inevitable.

Eventually, Mark performed our signature manoeuvre.

As it has been on many occasions, and will be again, he had to fit snow chains to complete the last eighteen inches of a journey. He reversed Kismet snug against the wall. There, she became an institution along with the Audi and the Heineken lorry, of which more later.

Still, with the village deserted and its central car park empty, who knew that a reneging Hotel Manger had failed to conduct us to the zenith of idiocy it was possible to achieve around the act of parking a caravan?

We checked inside Kismet. It was a joy to find her bone dry, with her re-connected battery fully charged and devoid of caustic ooze. Nevertheless, a surprise visit from the *carabinieri* soon dampened our spirits.

"You can't leave that there, mate. It's on private

land," was the effective translation of the tirade of "*Imposs-eee-bilis*" fired at Mark in Italian.

This was perplexing, not least because, to our knowledge, Kismet's neighbours, the Audi and the Heineken Lorry, had never moved in four years. A fellow seasonal vagabond, Rob, once commented,

"I took time lapse photos of that Audi as the snow gradually buried it. I used to post them on Facebook!"

I had done the same!

Since the *carabinieri* were the ones entrusted with enforcement, they were well placed to know that there was a travel ban in force across the whole of Italy. That only essential journeys were permitted. That we had to fill in a form to prove our journey was indeed essential, even to go and buy food. They knew that only one of us could sit in the car and, in order to be allowed back into Staffal, we had to carry our rental agreement for the apartment in our wallets.

But most of all – *there was no one there*! The car park was empty – and how, pray, could we make a seven-metre caravan disappear?

Even with the hotel closed, The Manager remained deaf to our mercy request to place Kismet back on his abandoned car park.

"But I love your wife and your four dogs," he told Mark, by way of compensation.

The *carabinieri* made a phone call, possibly for effect, and gave us special dispensation to leave Kismet where she was until April 3rd. They were adamant that restrictions on travel would not continue beyond that.

We had no idea whether we would be able to get out of Staffal, or if we could, that there would be anywhere to go. Social media was full of terrible stories of displaced motor homers, turfed off to fend for themselves as campsites closed all over the continent. Some were attacked or reported by locals, who blamed coronavirus on foreigners. Like us, with travel bans and ferry cancellations, they had nowhere to run.

Clearly, the *carabinieri* were bored. In more normal times, posing in their black uniforms and mirrored sunglasses kept them very busy. In Staffal, they often had the added complication of having to do all that on skis. They put a lot of effort into looking cool as they smoked cigarettes and caught a few rays while keeping order on the slopes. Denied all that frenetic activity, no wonder they were restless.

However, in the land of suntanned, skiing policemen, the most disappointing thing was to encounter the petty-minded 'jobsworth' mentality so common in the UK.

Pensavo fossi strafigo – I thought you were super cool.

But Blighty could still learn a few lessons from the Italians. Lockdown had caused shortages all over Britain because of panic buying. There was an inexplicable run on toilet paper. We could buy bog roll at will, any time we were allowed out of the house. In spite of the severity of her situation, Italy avoided all that hysterical selfishness.

I proposed that Brits should take a creative leaf out

of medieval monk François Rabelais' book and wipe their backsides on the neck of a goose.

In his book *Gargantua and Pantagruel,* M. R investigated a variety of lavatory paper alternatives, including "the shaggy hat," – which he reported as having good abstersive (cleansing) properties.

Regarding birds of the family *Anatidae,* however, he maintains, "... that of all torcheculs, arsewisps, bumfodders, tail-napkins, bunghole cleansers, and wipe-breeches, there is none in the world comparable to the neck of a goose, that is well downed, if you hold her head betwixt your legs. And believe me therein upon mine honour, for you will thereby feel in your nockhole a most wonderful pleasure, both in regard of the softness of the said down and of the temperate heat of the goose, which is easily communicated to the bum-gut and the rest of the inwards, in so far as to come even to the regions of the heart and brains."[2]

One thing was for sure, surviving lockdown called for creative solutions!

20. A LOCKDOWN LESSON FOR THE ENVIRONMENT AS EARTH DAY TURNS 50

"He is much more happy that at ease contemplates the universe as his own, and in it the sun and stars, the pleasing meadows, shades, groves, green banks, stately trees, flowing springs and the wanton windings of a river, than he that with fire and sword disturbs the world, and measures his possessions by the waste that lies around him."

I read these words decades ago in a book called *The Druid Way* by Philip Carr-Gomm and they still give me goosebumps. Written by John Aubrey in the 1600s, they were never more relevant than on the 50th anniversary of Earth Day.

First celebrated on 22nd April 1970, Earth Day is an annual global event designed to support environmental protection.

Although the reduction in air pollution over Italy during lockdown was certainly dramatic,[1] reports of swans and dolphins returning to Venice's canals were reputedly false.[2] Yet the effective shutdown of the world's economy because of coronavirus gave our planet a chance to breathe.

In Monte Rosa, the lack of human activity meant we had a few extraordinary encounters with nature, some more welcome than others.

Since mid-March, we had been unable to leave the house, except for one person to go alone to shop for food or seek non-existent medical attention. The Fab Four could accompany us into the garden for necessities, but that was the limit of our range. However, we found that an upside of being stuck is that you notice your surroundings so much more.

One afternoon at the beginning of April, Mother Nature sent us a real treat. As we sat on a boulder near the river, quietly savouring the sun's early spring warmth on our skin, a dark, winged behemoth appeared above the shoulder of Punta Telcio.

Like a fighter jet on exercises, the huge bird of prey swept down into the valley, then patrolled the forested flanks of the mountain. Of course, I didn't have my camera with me – we were just in the garden after all – but we lost ourselves in the moment, enraptured by a raptor. Time evaporated as the majestic creature glided effortlessly back and forth for what seemed like an age. Then it wheeled away on a thermal as suddenly and silently as it came.

"It seemed much bigger than a golden eagle, or

even a white-tailed sea eagle," I said to Mark. We'd been fortunate enough to experience both at close quarters in Scotland, on the Isle of Skye. White tailed sea eagles were a regular sight, while a golden eagle once took off from a crag almost beneath our feet. It was so close, we could hear the air in its feathers.

Later, when we looked it up, this bird's distinctive pale head and wedge-shaped tail blew its cover. It was unmistakably *il gipeto* – the bearded vulture (*Gypaetus barbatus*); Europe's rarest vulture.

With a wingspan of over 9 ft (2.7 m), *il gipeto* is also Europe's biggest bird of prey. It certainly dwarfs both the golden eagle, whose wingspan is 7.5 ft (2.3 m), and Britain's largest raptor, the white-tailed sea eagle's full 8 ft (2.5 m).

Il gipeto's other name, the *lammergier*, or lamb vulture, gives away the reason it was persecuted to extinction in the Alps and had to be re-introduced. As with the sea eagle, people misguidedly believed that these huge birds preyed on lambs and children. While there is some evidence for white-tailed eagles taking lambs (not children!), certainly, in the *lammergier's* case, this could not be further from the truth.

All vultures are scavengers and the bearded vulture never hunts live prey. *Il gipeto* is not even keen on meat; its diet is primarily bones taken from carcasses. It swallows small bones whole, but to get at the nutritious marrow, it breaks open larger bones by dropping them on to rocks. We had kept the dogs, especially little

Lani, close while watching the immense raptor. In hindsight, it was a relief to find out that our tiny girl was at precisely zero risk of being carried off in its talons!

Our *lammergier* was one of only twenty pairs in the whole of the Alps. This was our fourth full ski season in Monte Rosa. In total, we had spent over twelve months in the Gressoney valley, and this was our first vulture sighting. How lucky were we?!

Afterwards, I kept my camera glued to my person, but *il gipeto* had floated away and declined to perform an encore.

Rather less welcome visitors were the adders. The warm sunshine encouraged vipers to pop out of their dens. As we walked up the wooded bank at the back of our apartment block, Mark nearly stood on one serpent; motionless and basking peacefully in the sun. The following day, as he went to pick up a piece of litter next to a wall, another venomous viper slithered silently off into a crevice. Visible only when it moved, it was inches from his outstretched fingers.

Both encounters illustrate the good thing about adders; they are shy and prefer to avoid confrontation. They attack only when they feel threatened. Adders are rare and exquisite creatures. They are protected, so never harm an adder. However, we were concerned for the hounds, so on warmer days, Mark and I alternated as the advance party on Adder Patrol.

With prompt veterinary attention, adder bites are not fatal in most dogs, although we were mindful that an adder bite once nearly killed Oscar, who is bigger than The Fab Four combined. Stuck in isolation, an hour away from the nearest vet, we needed to avoid as many risks as possible. We emailed our Italian vet. She sent a prescription for an injection that could be administered in case of emergency, so we were a little more prepared. (In Monte Rosa, we collected all veterinary medication at the human pharmacy in Gressoney St. Jean!) Nevertheless, adder avoidance was definitely our favoured strategy.

As they come out of hibernation, the snakes are dozy and, being cold blooded, may be unable to move away quickly. This leaves them with no option but to strike to protect themselves. In the early spring, the venom, particularly in a large male, is sometimes stronger – which is why Oscar was so badly affected – so the best adder advice I can give is to steer clear!

Mark and I were running a book on the decline of the snow bridge, the remains of the huge avalanche which crossed the River Lys from our garden. We monitored it daily as it got narrower and lower.

As the mountains awakened, there were clearly a

few terrestrial hazards to avoid. After two weeks of sunshine, all traces of a three-day blizzard that had stranded us indoors at the end of March had gone, and the spring melt was well under way. On the far bank of the Lys, three colossal snow avalanches still blocked Footpath No.7, towards Monte Rosa. However, the tremendous crack and puff of smoke that we observed one evening was a rock avalanche. We watched a cascade of huge boulders thump and bounce down the sides of Telcio, leaving a wake of splintered stone and shattered tree trunks.

The immovable lockdown-lifting deadline of April 3rd, cited by The Italian Jobsworth, had come and gone. I gave Mark a sharp jab in the ribs when he said,

"We would be six weeks into our trip now!"

I found our confinement easier to bear by not thinking about what we were missing. We hoped Giuseppe Conte might relax the coronavirus restrictions on May 3rd, and that we would then be free to walk into the mountains. If we did, though, we would clearly need our wits about us!

Without the wild silence of isolation, we would never have seen the adders or *il gipeto*. It also gave me the chance to think about the wider lessons that the lockdown recovery could teach us about the environment.

I started this chapter by talking about pollution. A harsh twist in Italy came when studies found a potential link between air pollution and coronavirus mortality.[3] In China, estimates suggested that two months of cleaner air resulting from lockdown may have saved the lives of 4,000 under-fives and 73,000 adults over seventy.[4] This was just a tiny snapshot of one aspect of the impact that humanity has on the planet and its population. So, will these lessons from coronavirus make a lasting difference? I hope so.

Climate change is a hugely more complex issue than containing the spread of a novel virus. Something proven by the pandemic is that there *can* be a co-ordinated global reaction to a crisis.

The pandemic also initiated an unprecedented worldwide experiment in altering people's travel and work habits. Perhaps in future, remote or home working and video conferencing will be a more acceptable low-carbon alternative to commuting and business travel. And you never know, caravanning might become a cool and fashionable holiday trend to replace high-emission flights!

I wondered whether, having been forced to cope with less, due to shortages caused by stockpiling or the wider impacts of the pandemic, we might adjust our mindset regarding what consumer goods we need to survive – and be more careful about how much we waste. Separation from loved ones and denial of freedom was a massive wake-up call. It shone an incontrovertible floodlight on how small things that we take for granted are so much more integral to our happiness than material wealth.

But is my optimism misplaced? It is an uphill struggle to reform ingrained behaviours, but once restrictions are lifted and economies roar back to life, it is not inevitable that we will all return to our former bad habits.

Studies have shown that adapting to a new circumstance can cause enduring behavioural modification. For example, a 2018 study from Zurich University shows that, when given their cars back after having them substituted for free e-bike access, people drove less.[5] Coronavirus has imposed change upon us; maybe some of it will stick, particularly now that we have been granted a taste of what disaster on a global scale feels like.

There are certainly lessons to be learned from the coronavirus pandemic, and the first is to accept that if we look after our planet, it will look after us.

Our international connectedness was responsible for the rapid spread of the virus, but why did coronavirus happen? Research suggests that viruses transferring from animals to humans may be a direct consequence of humanity's destruction of biodiversity.[6] All pathogens evolve and adapt so, when you ravage their natural hosts or habitats, they need to look elsewhere. And as for that new host – well, it could be you-hoo!

Perhaps if we learn anything, it is that a few manageable changes we make as individuals could result in considerable environmental benefits. The majority of emissions responsible for climate change come from industry. Yet, even if we don't want to become active in pressuring our governments into adopting greener alternatives, we can each have an impact. We can all reduce our personal consumption of goods and fossil fuels and re-think the ways we live, work and travel.

I hope we do effect change, because the disruption to our lives caused by novel coronavirus is as nothing to what we will experience if we create the climate catastrophe that many predict could happen within our lifetimes. With coronavirus, or any future pandemics that we cause, at least we have some control. We can isolate to prevent the spread, and ultimately develop vaccines and more effective treatments for the disease. There is an end in sight.

However, once we reach the tipping point with the climate, it might make no difference what we do. There will be nowhere to hide. The likelihood is that we shall trigger irreversible changes to the equilibrium of the planet, and once that happens, humanity will have run out of options.

I found this quote on a beer bottle in Miami airport. Attributed to a speech by Chief Seattle in 1854, it foresaw the consequences of our disdain for nature and the potentially devastating impact of human activity on our world. Now, more than ever, we need to sit up and listen.

"What is a man without the beasts? If all the beasts

were gone, men would die from great loneliness of spirit, for whatever happens to the beasts also happens to man. All things are connected. This we know. Whatever befalls the Earth befalls the sons of the Earth. Man did not weave the web of life, he is merely a strand in it. Whatever he does to the web, he does to himself."

21. OUR FIRST TASTE OF FREEDOM ON STAR WARS DAY

May the Fourth be With You – as lockdown lifts a little in Italy...

Star Wars Day (May the Fourth be With You!) had special significance for us.

On May 4th, the Italian government relaxed coronavirus lockdown to allow us to go Out-Out. As in Properly Out. On a jaunt. We could now walk and exercise beyond the perimeter of our garden and drive together in the car, so long as we stayed within the boundaries of our region. The sun even had the grace to shine upon our first day of freedom.

We had both been restricted to the bounds our apartment since 20th March, and I had not left Staffal since lockdown started on the 8th. I had to resist the urge to motor all the way to Mont Blanc for no other reason than because we could!

We opted for a more modest excursion a few miles

down the mountain to Gressoney St. Jean. Our primary aim was to stock up on fresh produce at the newly re-opened Crai mini market and visit the pharmacy. On the face of it, the pharmacy trip was to score flea and tick medication for the dogs. However, the ulterior motive was to make use of their language skills.

The entire period of my Lockdown Life had incorporated a cavity in my upper right molar from the filling, which fell out the day after we were locked down. Since the pharmacists spoke excellent English, I wanted them to phone a dentist on my behalf.

It's not that my Italian language skills are not up to arranging a dental appointment. As with grocery shopping, they are simply inadequate for dealing with the machine-gun barrage of wordage that is inevitably fired back in reply.

Begging, "*Più lentamente*" – more slowly has no effect.

Phrases such as, "*Sono inglese*" – I am English or worse, "*Parli inglese?*" – Do you speak English? telegraph a potential hassle factor so great to phone operatives that they usually slam down the receiver straight away.

My emails to dental practitioners throughout the region had gone unanswered. In hindsight, perhaps it was a mistake to preface them with "*Sono una donna Inglese*" – I am an English woman... So, Plan C was to go undercover, via the pharmacist.

It was strange to encounter no roadblock at the roundabout in Gressoney la Trinité. No one demanded forms to justify our movements. This was freedom on an unprecedented scale!

Stocked with groceries and on a promise of 5 p.m. for collection of doggie medication, we set off on *La Passegiata Della Regina* – The Queen's Walk.

This was the route taken by Margherita, Queen of Savoy, from her fairy-tale *Castel Savoia* into the village of St. Jean. It is one of our favourite walks too; a pathway high above the valley floor that winds through a secret woodland of larch, pine, and a labyrinth of giant, mossy boulders.

We started on the banks of the chattering River Lys, heading towards the hamlet of Tschemenoal. There, we could cross the main road, the SR44, to join the *Passegiata*, which runs along the opposite side of the valley.

For the first time ever, after crossing the road, we found and followed the official footpath route. The sign was never very clear and the true path looked like it led into someone's backyard. We snaked through Tschemenoal's maze of narrow, cobbled streets, between the ancient, blackened timbers of the traditional Walser houses, known as *stadels*. This cobbled revelation was not only more scenic than the field we had previously crossed, but also strategically avoided the bubbling lake of farm slurry, the colour of a *caffè latte*, that lurked malevolently in the corner. No longer frozen solid, the muck midden was delightfully viscous, clinging and malodorous; Paradise Found for our poodle-based pooches! (*Pudel* is German for poodle, related closely to the English word 'puddle'. Poodles were bred as water retrievers, which is also reflected in their French name *caniche* – derived from *canard* – duck.)

Curiously, a viewing bench overlooked the midden. Perhaps they designed it especially for puddle hounds to gaze longingly when denied a splash in the sludge – or for their owners to sit down and recover from the horror when they did!

The avalanche chutes we had crossed during our early winter walks there were much reduced. However, as we clambered over the debris of large boulders and tree trunks that remained after the melt, we remained convinced that the best way to survive an avalanche is not to get caught in one. We inhaled deeply as we trudged through the woods; the warm scent of pine in our nostrils and the trill of birdsong in our ears spelled one thing. Spring!

While picking up supplies at Crai, we noticed that Café Pinter next door was open, but for takeaway only. Since we were Out-Out, we went wild and promised ourselves a coffee on the way back.

From the *Passegiata*, we dropped down to Lake Gover in the public park. It sits beneath the cliffs that are home to Via Ferrata Jòsé Angster, a cabled rock climb along the precipice. Denied the farm slurry and with no one around to complain, we found a stick and treated The Pawsome Foursome to a cooling game of fetch in the crystalline turquoise waters. Their antics shattered the perfect reflection of the snow-covered

Monte Rosa massif, framed by emerald green parkland. A few thousand feet lower than snow-bound Staffal, the new season had arrived much earlier in St. Jean.

At Café Pinter, we had a *cappucino* each. To honour the spirit of 'takeaway', we sat on a bench in the sun a few yards away, where Caroline and Graham's British neighbours joined us at a safe distance. We had a conversation. With actual people. For the first time in months. It was amazing!

And so, we returned to Staffal up the hairpins replete with fresh food, tick medication and a first contact with other humans. The only thing missing was the dental appointment. The message came back; the *dentista* was taking emergencies only.

Since I couldn't possibly feign agony or fib, me and my cavity looked set to enjoy a few more lockdown adventures together. I had a smile on my face from my first taste of freedom in nearly two months. If only Phil (my cavity) could have known what excitement was about to come...

22. HOW THE GREATEST ROCK CLIMBER IN THE ALPS WAS SAVED BY THE HUNTER KING & A POACHER

An extraordinary tale of survival!

As spring began to colour in the scenery, a few summer migrants arrived in the Alps. House martins got busy under our eaves, while the meadows were a-flutter with crag martins and wheatears.

Wheatears are one of my favourite birds, and if you want to know why, all I can say is tits, bustards, shags and boobies.

I love 'em all because they fall into the same pleasing category of birds with rude-sounding names. The word 'wheatear' has nothing to do with cereal crops. It actually derives from the 16th-Century term 'whiteers', meaning 'white-arse'. In flight, its distinctive white rump makes it very easy to spot, while simultaneously providing a secret snigger to those of us blessed with a puerile sense of humour.

When the news reported that US President Donald

Trump had recommended injecting disinfectant and irradiating people to combat coronavirus because, although he was not a doctor, he knew stuff, I didn't think my day could get any better.[1] (*Don't do this! I thought a small child, never mind the US President, would know that methods of disinfection suitable for surfaces, such as irradiation and bleach, are very harmful just in contact with the skin, and bleach is certainly not safe to inject...*)

However, we got our most amazing wildlife encounter yet, and it happened just over the river from our garden.

In Staffal, the thaw was well under way and the vibrant spring grass was beginning to come through. Had the remains of the avalanche that formed the snow bridge crossing the River Lys not been there, we might never have seen them, they were so well camouflaged. But a herd of *stambecchi* (Alpine ibex – *Capra ibex*) walked straight into the village.

Despite long periods spent in Monte Rosa, my first and only *stambecco* sighting had happened what seemed like aeons ago, back in February. From a ski lift, I saw a few black dots crossing a snowfield on the mountainside. I was thrilled!

I have seen ibex in other resorts, but only ever in the far distance. I often wondered how such a large animal could be so difficult to spot, but their golden coats render them invisible among the grass and rocks. We would not have spotted this small herd had we not looked up at the moment they crossed the ribbon of snow.

Lo stambecco, the Alpine ibex, is revered in the area; you will find bronze statues of them all over the valley. In the 18th century, folk believed they had magical powers, and the form of *Capra ibex* often represents Capricorn, the tenth sign of the zodiac.

Their sharp-edged, concave hooves allow them to cling on to impossibly steep terrain. The mountain goats pictured defying gravity to lick salt from the stones of the near-vertical face of the Cingino Dam in Piedmont are ibex. Justifiably, they take the title of 'the greatest rock climbers in the Alps'.

Amid all this veneration, it shocked me to learn that, in the 18th and 19th century, this iconic creature was hunted almost to extinction in the Alps. Ibex have a habit of seeking refuge on steep terrain rather than running away. This made them easy targets, particularly with the advent of firearms. Hunters sought ibex for meat, although unsurprisingly, their magnificent, curved horns, which can be up to three feet (1 m) long, made great trophies. Tobacco and snuff boxes carved from ibex horn were highly prized, but in folk medicine, the *stambecco* was also a walking pharmacy. Healers credited many of its body parts with extraordinary properties.

In a small proportion of ibex, the arteries leaving the heart form a cross, which 'ossifies' with a bony deposit in some older animals. This 'heart cross' was a charm believed to improve male virility and protect soldiers from a violent death.

Powdered ibex horn could allegedly cure hysteria,

cramps and poisoning. Some claimed an ibex heel bone was an aphrodisiac, while ibex blood supposedly cured bladder stones. A drinking vessel made from ibex horn could protect the drinker from poison; a powerful attribute shared with the horn of only one other creature – a unicorn.

Ironically, a prolific hunter and a poacher saved 'The King of the Alps' from extinction. By the end of the 19th century, the only remaining ibex population in the world was in the Gran Paradiso, the royal hunting reserve of King Vittorio Emanuele II. Vittorio, the first king of a unified Italy since the 6th century, was no conservationist. Known as *il re cacciatore* – The Hunter King, he slaughtered vast numbers of ibex in his time. The interior of his castle at Sarre is decorated with thousands of ibex horns.

The few animals remaining in his royal reserve were protected from poaching – except for three kids purloined by professional poacher, Gabriele Bérard and his son Giuseppe. Two female and one male, the kidnappers (see what I did there?!) smuggled them into Switzerland's St. Gallen Zoo.

Ibex had been extinct in Switzerland for a century but when asked, the Italians refused to supply the zoo with any pure-bred specimens. So, these three stolen babies initiated the reintroduction of ibex into Switzerland.

In 1922, Gran Paradiso became Italy's first national park. The park's symbol is the ibex.

Now, thousands of ibex roam the Alps, descended

from approximately sixty *stambecchi* who were the sole survivors in the Gran Paradiso. The problem for ibex is that this near-extinction and re-population from so few animals means their genetic diversity is not as robust as it might be.

The ibex is also particularly sensitive to climate change. *Stambecchi* are adapted to the extreme cold of a high, mountain environment and struggle to regulate their body temperature in the heat. Research shows their need to keep cool by ascending to higher altitudes, where the vegetation is less nutritious, outweighs the ibex's drive to find food. This adversely affects their ability to build up the reserves they require to survive the harsh Alpine winter.

I hope the changing climate is something we can address. After returning this magnificent creature from the brink of extinction, it would be such a shame to lose The King of the Alps once again.

I was buzzing for a week from this amazing wildlife encounter, so I hope beyond hope that there will be *stambecchi* in Staffal for future generations to enjoy.

23. 8,000 FT WALKIES

Never call a Cavapoo frou-frou...

"Did someone switch off the Matrix?" I asked Mark when he opened the bedroom's wooden shutters on the new day.

In a perfect metaphor for coronavirus lockdown, the entire world beyond our garden had vanished. All we could see was a grey emptiness; as though we were the only remaining oasis of life, and the rest of creation had been erased.

There had been more than two feet (69 cm) of snow in the forecast, but at village level, it pelted down as rain all day. No pups wanted to go outside, and since we were almost out of data, there was no Netflix or internet for us. Once again, we had become a hibernation, with our recently restored freedom removed by the weather. We were all just so *bored*.

"If tomorrow's nice, we'll do a proper walk..." we promised our pooches.

The following morning, as the surrounding mountains held the banks of cloud at bay, the shutters opened on Staffal as a bright oasis of sunshine enclosed within a steep stockade of grey. Thankfully, the wider world had re-materialised, albeit in monochrome.

Rather than just warming himself on the stones in the wall, the adder, our now familiar personal barometer, poised motionless on the ground in hunting mode. We kept our fur babies at a safe distance and determined to head for the hills.

We joined Footpath No. 1, which rose up the forested bank directly behind our apartments. It was a well-marked trail, and we knew we could descend quickly if the weather came in. Besides, I had promised Dad a special photograph...

As children, my brothers and I spent most family holidays in a remote forestry cottage in an obscure Lake District valley. Ennerdale was my first spiritual home. The cottage, four miles down a private track, nestled in greenery with a view of the iconic summits of Pillar and Great Gable, two of the UK's highest peaks. It was a special place, and its lonely grandeur truly captured my heart. When I phoned Dad at the weekend, I described the location of our Italian apartment,

"We're the last building in the Lys Valley, a bit like

Black Sail Youth Hostel at the head of Ennerdale; right underneath the mountains!"

"But do you have drumlins?" Dad asked.

As children, drumlins terrified us. We knew they were to be found somewhere near Black Sail, a few miles away from our friendly abode at Gillerthwaite. Their territory was the bleak, treeless, and barren head of the valley, where Pillar and Great Gable's dark imposing crags and pinnacles reared malevolently above.

Our fertile young minds needed no encouragement. Drumlins were clearly terrifying monsters. Mum and Dad never enlightened us; the threat of drumlins proved a useful means of keeping three boisterous and inquisitive siblings from wandering too far from base. It worked perfectly until we studied glaciation at school. Then, we discovered that drumlins are nothing more than oval hills, carved out of silt, and deposited by a passing glacier.

"We don't have drumlins, but we do have some lovely lateral moraines," another form of glacial debris. "I'll get you a photo!"

We departed footpath No. 1 where it forked left to Bettolina, and turned right to cross a wooden bridge over the River Lys. Staying high, we joined Footpath No. 7, above the tiny three-house summer hamlet of Courtlys. There, we saw some of our friends, the *stambecchi* – Alpine ibex, and the disappearing butt of some small furry creature. It might have been a marmot, although its dark fur and long tail suggested it was something more akin to a polecat.

"Shall we drop back into Staffal from here?"

Since the sun was warming our backs and we were all loving being beyond the limits of the apartment, we continued upwards. As we rose high above the River Lys and emerged from the shade of the larch woodland, the path was mostly clear, although we still had a few snow patches to cross.

One of the principal hazards of snow slopes is that if you lose your footing and start to slide, it's almost impossible to stop. In most circumstances, self-arrest is an unattainable fantasy, so halting a fall is usually delivered by other means, such as slamming into a boulder, or falling over a cliff. Mark discovered another hazard. As he stepped on one snow patch, his legs disappeared up to his hips!

Ahead, the giant snow-covered 2.5-mile high (4,000 m) peaks of the Monte Rosa massif hove in and out of view through the clouds.

The path afforded us fantastic views of the off-piste ski itinerary of Bettolina Bassa on the hillside opposite. We could clearly see the two distinct lines of descent we had taken through a hanging side valley when we skied it with a guide a few years ago. One benefit of walking in a ski resort is that it's a perfect way to get your bearings, and check out off-piste routes.

At the next junction where the path divided, a sign promised the *Sorgenti del Lys* – Sources of the Lys – was only half an hour away. It seemed rude not to! Had we taken the right fork, footpath No. 7C led up the Vallone di Salza – a back country ski route yet to be ticked off our bucket list.

7C's ultimate destination was the peak Punta Alta Luce / Hochlicht (High Light) at 3,185 m, along with the iconic mountain refuges of Gnifetti and Mantova on the massif itself. Like most footpaths in the Lys valley, the only way was up, but on a glacier at 3,647 and 3,498 m respectively (just below 12,000 ft), the refuges were a little beyond the scope of our unequipped afternoon stroll.

In Courtlys, Ruby had excelled herself. At 6,500 ft (2,000 m), our little bog-monster discovered an oozing patch of marsh to paddle in. Then, in the hollow beneath a tongue of lateral moraine, our water-baby shot into a small lake, unperturbed by the lacy fringe of ice that rimmed her personal paddling pool.

Then we climbed.

Lateral moraine is silt and other rocky detritus pushed to the side by an advancing glacier. We ascended the steep sides until we reached its knife-edge top. Cloud bubbled up around us, but we were now determined to arrive at our destination.

"It's like making a push for the top of Everest!" Mark said.

Immovable obsession with reaching a target is how many mountaineering accidents happen, but unlike on Everest, we had a clear path ahead and could descend very swiftly if the weather deteriorated. The sign on the footpath implied we could make it back to our base camp, Staffal, within forty-five minutes.

There was no one else around. We had the magnificent mountain wilderness to ourselves. Until I went for a pee.

I squatted in a prominent spot overlooking the entire valley and bragged to Mark, "I'm having an ironic pee, since we're up here all alone. This is my loo with a view!"

"I wouldn't be too sure!" he replied. "There's a bloke down there by the glacier lake!"

"What?!"

I thought he was kidding. Although hidden from view while I had my trousers around my ankles, when I shot up, I was astounded to see that Mark was not fibbing! A lean, tanned type in shorts, with a halo of curly black hair, arose from where he had crouched to take photos of the Monte Rosa glaciers across the meltwater lake. He hauled a rucksack on to his back, gave us a quick wave, then set off to descend at a jog. At a jog! I mean, that was just showing off!

The final ascent was steep enough to warrant cables in the rock to offer a steadying hand hold, although it was still a path, not the sort of sheer face you would encounter on a cabled 'via ferrata' rock climb. Mark and I stayed close together so that any boulders we dislodged would not land on the other's head. Ruby was less careful, and sent a reasonably sized pebble bouncing down the hillside to miss Rosie's rump by a whisker. A sixth sense seemed to prompt Rosie to move out of the way at the last moment. It wasn't life threatening, but it would have smarted!

The darkening sky began to look ominous, but we passed a cairn whose sign channelled one of my favourite Stranglers' songs; *Five Minutes and You're Almost There*. I'm not sure The Stranglers have ever been five minutes from the *Sorgenti del Lys,* but at that stage, we couldn't give up.

The view, a forbidding moonscape of shattered rock, ice, and cold green water, was brooding and impressive amid the cloud. Narrow ribbons of white water cascaded over the cliff at one end of the glacial lake – the sources of the River Lys.

Pride stirred inside me. I could not believe the pups had made it all that way on their little legs. I took a photo of Lani, a tiny toy poodle cross, at 7,930 ft (2,417 m). The mighty glaciers and seracs of Monte Rosa loomed behind her and, as The Pawsome Foursome did their puppy pose at the summit cairn, the wind was strong enough to lift her ears out at right angles, like aeroplane wings.

The route back was a re-trace of our steps, but with a different view. Instead of a moody Monte Rosa massif, the green, sun-kissed Valle del Lys spread before us.

Soon, we left the desolate, rocky amphitheatre of high mountains and glacial debris at the head of the valley and re-entered Staffal's friendly little puddle of warmth. On our return journey, Courtlys still bathed in sunshine and was surrounded by an army. We counted more than forty *stambecchi* grazing contentedly on the emerald green pastures around the empty stone lodges. When I stopped with Kai to admire the herd, my ear worm was an homage to Elvis Costello; we were *Watching the Stambecchi*. (Detectives!)

There were plenty of clear streams and rivulets for our pooches to drink from, but since we had not intended quite such a long trek, Mark and I had no water for ourselves. We were certainly ready for a cuppa as we dropped back into the meadows around Staffal.

Lani jumped up and scratched at Mark's legs.

"Ow!" – our sweet little girl always demands affection with menaces.

He picked her up for a cuddle, and carried her back to base. The Pawsome Foursome always run about three times the distance we walk and, after climbing 1,850 ft (564 m) at altitude, I think her petite puppy paws had earned it!

We have an active lifestyle; an important reason we chose Cavapoos was the breeder telling us, "They can take as much exercise as you can throw at them."

The Fab Four certainly proved that.

Never underestimate a Cavapoo. They may be fluffy, cuddly and look like teddy bears, but as I said at the start – never call a Cavapoo frou-frou!

24. A WANDER WITH WILD FLOWERS & WILDLIFE

7,000 ft Walkies!

My dad is a mathematician and maintains there is no such thing as coincidence. During our weekly phone call, he said he was watching *Groundhog Day,* a film in which actor, Bill Murray, re-lives the same day over and over. After we spoke, Mark and I put on the first film that popped up on Netflix. It was *The Edge of Tomorrow,* starring Tom Cruise, and the plot was *Groundhog Day* with aliens.

Star Trek – The Next Generation helped us fill in time during our isolation. The following day, after seventy-nine episodes, we happened to have reached Series 5, Episode 18. Called *Cause and Effect*, it was *Groundhog Day* aboard the star ship Enterprise.

Surely, the gods were just rubbing it in, making us live *Groundhog Day* in film as well as reality! Yet, the big difference between Lockdown Life and *Groundhog Day* was that at least the scene outside changed.

In the film, Bill Murray's window opened daily on the same snowy landscape, although he was permitted social contact and could stray beyond the picket fence surrounding his garden. For us, seventy-two days into lockdown, the Alpine scenery had moved decisively from winter to spring. Even the thick snow on the bottom of Moos, the sunny piste opposite our apartment, had almost disappeared.

Although restrictions were somewhat relaxed, we had still seen virtually no one and, because of the weather, could not always get outside. After four years touring in a caravan, Mark and I were accustomed to spending all our time together in a small space, but even we felt emotionally drained.

Our upbeat approach to isolation had worn thin. What faced us now was a daily battle to remain positive. I struggled to summon the enthusiasm to read, or even enjoy passive entertainment from the TV. You'd think for an author, lockdown would be the most perfect writer's retreat, but in the absence of any stimulation, creativity and motivation deserted me. I felt bereft by the loss of my passion. With our globetrotting tendencies, Mark and I yearned for freedom and struggled with our incarceration.

It was difficult to comprehend. After all, we were comfortable, safe and surrounded by beauty and nature. Yet our confinement revealed an empirical truth about human nature and also exposed our own hunger for variety.

People need people. Observations from orphanages[1] have shown that babies and children provided with every material comfort, but denied affection and human contact, invariably become ill or die. Studies also show that in adults, such deprivation causes stress, depression and declining health.[2]

I lived in the house where I was born until I left for university at seventeen. At thirty-five, when I met Mark, I had lived all over the UK and moved home twenty-two times. Twenty-two moves in eighteen years is perhaps a reflection of my restless nature!

With uncertainty hanging over our travel plans, we committed to stay in the apartment until the end of June; four months beyond when our itchy feet had urged us to leave.

Although we could now go outside the boundary of our residence to walk, the weather was mixed, and the forecasts contradictory. Naturally, we did what any self-respecting windsurfers would do, and always believed the best one!

One sunny morning, we decided the most appropriate therapy to appease our vagabond cravings was to get high.

In November, before the winter snows came, we did a gorgeous, circular walk to the chapel of St. Anna. At 7,145 ft (2,178 m), the tiny white shrine nestles beneath the imposing, double peak of the Rothorn, and offers a commanding, panorama of the entire Lys valley. St. Anna and her husband, Joachim, were Jesus' grandparents.

When it is open, in fewer than two minutes, the Staffal to St. Anna cable car will whisk you to within a whisper of the chapel and its carved wooden statue of the saint. May is closed season anyway; Monte Rosa opens for the summer from mid-June to the end of August, so even without a lockdown, we had no choice but to make the ascent under our own steam.

We set out up the zigzag. Birdsong and the rush of waterfalls had replaced winter's snow muffled silence. Vibrant woodland blooms splashed colour over what had been a glittering but sterile blanket of white.

Our ascent granted a perfect vantage towards the head of the valley, and an overview of our route to the Sources of the Lys. The knife-edge lateral moraines on either side of the vale were well defined, and a sunny spotlight picked out the stone cottages in the emerald meadows of Courtlys. If we squinted, we could just make out a miniscule blob – the cairn we'd walked to on top of the ridge.

In the sunshine, the ripple of white domes that form the Monte Rosa massif were in full view, and almost free of cloud. The rounded, eastern peak of Lyskamm, rising to 14,852 ft (4,527 m), made our breathless ascent to nearly 8,000 ft (2,400 m) look puny and insignificant. Lyskamm is not even the tallest summit on the massif; that honour goes to Dufourspitze at 15,203 ft (4,624 m).

The pastures at the top of the zigzag were alive

with wild flowers; primrose-yellow Alpine anemones and dark purple trumpets of gentians. Like confetti strewn outside a cathedral after a wedding, sky blue forget-me-nots, speedwell, and the sunny four-petalled faces of tormentil littered the grass, along with a million other tiny pinpricks of colour. Once we reached the plateau at the top, Mark changed our plan.

"Rather than turn left towards the chapel, why don't we climb up to the right, towards the refuge on Alpe Sitten? From there, we will be able to see whether the route to the Salero Lakes, *Laghetti Salero*, is free of snow. If it is, we can walk there another day."

Our near-vertical scramble up the grassy bank was rewarded. As Mark quietly beckoned me upwards to observe a herd of ibex, a marmot ran across our field of view. Then, a familiar span of giant glossy wings blotted out the sun. *Il gipeto* made a few passes above us, on a constant quest for bones to break on the rocks.

Distracted by the wildlife, we realised our numbers were depleted. Lani and Lampo were nowhere to be seen. When we caught sight of them, they were both miles away and miles below, chasing who-knows-what on the grassland in front of the cable car. After they galloped up the steep hill to join us, we sat for a while on the abandoned terrace outside the *rifugio* to give their little limbs a rest.

We started our descent from Sitten on the black ski run, Nera. After the initial slope, the piste turned sharply left into a precipitous, north-facing gulley, which still retained a treacherous covering of slippery frozen snow. I mentioned the peril of snow slopes previously. For safety, we crossed rough ground to rejoin the zigzag; our route of ascent.

When Mark and I finally sat down with a cuppa back at the apartment, our spirits were lifted. We had chosen the correct weather forecast and succeeded in getting high.

Recently, we had seen marmots and ibex on most of our walks. If Groundhog Day meant repeated sightings of glorious scenery and rare wildlife, perhaps we should not complain.

Fresh air and the beauty of nature are good for the soul, and a swift re-setting of your altitude never hurts.

25. THE DREAM HOUSE AT CIALVRINO

How finding our dream house made us realise we're not ready to abandon our nomadic lifestyle!

In keeping with the rest of our life, the walk did not work out as planned.

After several strenuous hikes above 7,000 ft, we decided to go flat.

Only that morning, the British Government scattered more caltrops across our road home to the UK. In a spectacular feat of closing-the-door-months-after-the-horse-bolted, they announced plans to introduce a compulsory, fourteen-day quarantine for anyone entering Britain. Unlike all the other rulings, which were mere guidelines, this was framed in criminal law. As such, it was considerably more severe than the isolation measures in place for someone who had tested positive for COVID-19!

Our situation hadn't changed; our property was

still rented, our relatives still vulnerable, and campsites still closed. With no address to self-isolate and a £1,000 fine for breaking the terms, what could we do?

A return from Italy to the UK looked further away than ever.

A walk in Gressoney St. Jean to incorporate a trip to the newly re-instated weekly market volunteered a strand of serendipity. In the local Walser dialect, *La Strada Lombarda* is named after us! *Lambertschgasso*.

Despite the promise of Valdobbia's waterfall at the end of what our guidebook described as 'a mule track used by merchants coming from Lombardy', both we and Footpath 14 got off to an unpromising start.

"They wouldn't direct a footpath around the back of the sports centre!" I rationalised, even though a signpost next to the *Sporthaus* suggested otherwise.

A riot of weeds backed on to the centre.

"It's completely overgrown. There's no clear route through there," I said, just as I spied a wooden bridge over a stream.

"That seems like the obvious way, but it leads in the opposite direction from the Valdobbia cascade..."

We followed the narrow, stony trail. It was not well-used and climbed steeply through a woodland. I said to Mark,

"This looks far too tricky, even for mules."

As he perused the wrong bit of the map without his glasses, Mark remained convinced that it would join a higher path, which would ultimately arc back towards our destination.

We clambered over the trunks of several huge fallen trees and reached a boulder avalanche. Beyond was what appeared to be someone's private *ménage* of horse jumps, so we gave up and turned around.

Back at the sports centre, we slapped our foreheads as we spied a faded yellow arrow painted on the concrete wall. The footpath did indeed take the scenic route through the weeds and past the industrial hoses and air conditioning units that, in less dystopian times, would serve the deserted leisure centre. After wading through waist-high undergrowth, we spotted the start of the mule track at the far end of the centre. It had a barrier across and a large sign that declared it *Chiuso*.

It was closed.

Muttering to ourselves, we returned to Big Blue, via the concrete car park at the front of the *Sporthaus*.

"Why don't they just start the footpath at that end of the sports centre? The weeds and aircon units really add nothing to the walk. The car park is easier underfoot and so much more picturesque..."

Grumpily, we all clambered back into the van. Four doggy faces glowered at us,

"You drove us down twenty minutes of hairpins for THAT!"

We promised them the brief circumnavigation of a concrete sports centre was not 'it' for walkies. If only we could have guessed what was to come.

"Let's drive up to *Castel Savoia*. There are some footpaths up there," I suggested.

At the very least, the pretty *Passegiata della Regina* –

The Queen's Walk started there. I studied the map as we drove, flung from side to side on more switchbacks, and spotted a circular route above the castle that we had not done before. It appeared about the right length.

"If we go up Footpath No. 2, it is a gradual ascent, with a stiffer descent down Footpath 3."

My itinerary seemed to cross the contour lines at an angle. Viewing them through varifocals in a jolting vehicle, they looked quite widely spaced. I didn't pay too much attention to the altitude markers.

The initial climb was rather steeper than I anticipated, but the beauty of the forest distracted me. Great mossy boulders, one with a full-sized larch tree growing out of it, littered our way. We felt transported.

"I feel like I am abroad!" I said to Mark.

"You are abroad. You're in Italy!" he replied.

"You know what I mean. I feel like I am somewhere else."

Mark agreed that the moss-covered landscape and dappled light reminded him of forests we had walked through on our travels in Germany and Eastern Europe.

As the woodland ended, we crossed St. Jean's Leonardo David ski run, now adorned in a livery of bright spring green, rather than its shroud of winter white. A bijou hut with a rusting corrugated iron roof flew the Italian *tricolore* and Union Jack flags. It had the most glorious view down to the village, thousands of feet below.

"That would do me!" I said to Mark. He agreed. If we do ever move back 'in the brick', our dream is a tiny house in a wonderful location. However, if lockdown has taught us anything, it's that, five years into our three-year road trip, we're not yet ready to settle by the fireside in one place.

Further ascent up a forest track wound past *Ristorante Cialvrino* and a large white church with a tin roof. There, the footpath appeared to merge with the narrow mountain road, although the map did not agree. We studied the map carefully, but opted to believe our eyes, not the map, and joined the road. Even that was pretty. A few glorious little houses clung to its vertiginous sides, hidden in *Hansel and Gretel* woodland. Gaps through the trees afforded a periodic glimpse of giant waterfalls opposite, free falling thousands of feet down entire mountainsides. One of them was the elusive *Cascata Valdobbia,* so at least we saw it, albeit from a distance!

A little more map confusion ensued where Footpath 2 (the road) joined Footpath W, whose signpost claimed it was Footpath 1W. With no other paths around, we deduced it must be the right way, so we followed it upwards and at once, found ourselves in paradise. A gorgeous two storey *stadel* house greeted us. Chips of mica in its fish-scale stone roof tiles glittered gold in the sun.

Alone on a plateau, surrounded by a meadow filled with purple orchids,* it commanded a three-hundred-and-sixty-degree panorama of the Lys valley, with uninterrupted views to the immovable snow-covered blockade of Monte Rosa at its head. It took our breath away; not least because it displayed a sign saying it was for rent!

Considerable uncertainty lingered over when travel might return to normal across Europe. We'd emailed one French campsite, who thought they might re-open in mid-June. Although Germany was lifting restrictions, we wondered whether they would welcome a couple of Brits from the alleged coronavirus hotspot tramping around their castles and the Black Forest. With our return to the UK seeming more unlikely than ever, an idea formed. Perhaps we could hole up there instead?

But if we thought the first *stadel* was good, the main event was just above. My camera ran out of battery as we ascended to the two little chalets on the next level. Snapping away in excitement, I completely forgot I carried a spare! Their views were even better, and their size much more in keeping with our love of tiny living spaces. It was like a dream come true. We could really see ourselves there; high in the mountains and engulfed by beauty.

It was hard to drag ourselves away, but the path beckoned us into another magical woodland. Surrounded by delicate buttery Alpine anemones and the shiny, green leaves of myrtle bushes, we picked our way over chattering streams and through boulder gardens formed by ancient rock falls. With dramatic snow-covered peaks forming a monumental backdrop, views in every direction caused us to gasp in awe.

At the start of our walk, we had passed a signboard showcasing children's drawings of Gune, which suggested it was a destination of note en route. At 6,135 ft (1,870 m), Gune was the high point of our route in more ways than one. That it warranted its own signboard elevated our expectations.

Our tired legs noted my lack of attention to the difference in altitude between Gune and our starting point.

A 1,444 ft (440 m) climb was anything but the flat walk we had promised ourselves. But there was still no sign of Gune. After the many map-based confusions, the butterfly of doubt unfurled its wings and began to flutter behind my diaphragm. If we got lost in the hills, no one knew we were there, and there was no chance of rescue. I consoled myself that we had passed under the ski lift, so our worst-case-scenario was the glaringly obvious descent down the wide, green swathe of the Leonardo David piste.

On one section of the path, we passed a high-rise city of giant ants' nests. (Giant nests, not giant ants!)

"Maybe this is like Gune. An anty-climax!" I said to Mark.

Just from the groan, I knew my pun had hit the spot. It was unnecessary for Mark to add,

"No. THAT was the anti-climax..."

Gune turned up eventually, exactly where we had expected it; immediately before we began our descent on Footpath 3. Gune appeared to be a rocky, grassy bluff with a very sheer front face. In a particularly verdant part of the forest, it was indeed an enchanted spot, worthy of children's drawings. Spring green vegetation contrasted with the striated gold and copper-coloured boulders. The rocks were all a-sparkle as tiny flakes of mica collected sunbeams to throw back at us like a glittering sprinkle of confetti. A dead larch formed a lofty black totem pole, with bracket fungi texturing its trunk. From its broken skeletal branches, festoons of lacy grey-blue lichen wafted in the breeze.

I was relieved to have chosen Footpath 3 for the descent rather than the ascent – and not only because the views were better going clockwise. The other way around, we would have turned our backs on the glory of Monte Rosa, but the precipitous down-climb made our thighs shake. Going up would have turned them to jelly. We emerged at a deserted timber yard, close to where we'd parked Big Blue.

There, Mark stopped me suddenly with his hand on my shoulder. Almost in a whisper, he said, "Jax. Look..."

On every walk recently, we had spotted rare wildlife. I scanned the deserted yard carefully. The hushed reverence in Mark's voice suggested at least a troupe of trumpet-bearing marmots in heraldic dress, mounted upon gilded ibex, as a bearded vulture hovered overhead, with a fluttering *tricolore* clasped in its talons.

My gaze came to rest on a magnificent beast: bullnosed and muscular, shimmering as it stood creamy-white and perfectly still in the sultry afternoon haze. A Volvo N10 truck, motionless on six oversized, knobbly tyres; its sturdy back laden with the trunks of at least twenty full-grown trees.

"I've got to go and look at that!" I said, and rushed over to marvel at the classic lines of the truck. It was the first time I had ever knowingly met a Volvo N10, a sister of The Beast from Belgium we had bought unseen in January.

On paper, I knew she was ten metres (33 ft) long, and her cab four metres (13 ft) tall. Yet, until you stand next to such a monster, you have no concept of how such dimensions feel in reality. When I placed the palm of my hand on her, it was like touching the solid and dependable shoulder of a carthorse. She exuded an aura of power, sun-warmed steel, and Scandinavian reliability. As I ran my hands along the length of her chassis, some of the trepidation fell away. She was too big and too heavy – the sweet spot for an overland truck is cited as 10 tonnes – but I could tell our new home would look after us.

Back at base, I checked out *Baita Cialvrina* on the Estate Agent's web page. With a price tag of €200 per night, our summer dreams swiftly shattered. A week amid those Alpine meadows would cost more than three months in our little apartment under the mountain in Staffal. Nevertheless, it's always nice to dream, because occasionally, dreams do come true.

The second dream home we saw, the Volvo N10,

was slowly becoming a reality. And in any case, a dream home that could travel overland to Mongolia was much more our style!

* **Orchis mascula** – I thought you would like to know that the Latin name for the early purple orchid, *Orchis mascula*, means 'masculine' or 'virile' due to its roots; two tubers which apparently look like testicles. Known as 'Adam and Eve Root', in some cultures, extracts were used in love potions. A nutritious flour called *salep* or *sachlav* made from the dried and ground tubers was a popular ingredient in drinks and desserts in the former Ottoman Empire.

26. ENGLISH ECCENTRICS & INTERNATIONAL RESCUE

Random worries & a busy week!

It was a mission of mercy.

"Have you bought your quad yet?" Tomasz asked as he and his young family ambled past us on the zigzag path, next to the Oagre Chapel. Tanned and fit from a youth filled with healthy mountain sports, we had first met Tomasz a few days previously, on our morning dog walk.

Rosie had bowled up to him in his shed behind *Rezidenza Le Marmotte*. He worked as a *pisteur*, and was exchanging snow tracks for wheels on his quad bike. We called Rosie back, apologised, and explained that she was only being friendly. Tomasz had smiled and summed up the loneliness of Lockdown Life in two sentences,

"Don't worry. It's a relief just to *talk* to someone!"

Mark and I were in the market for an All-Terrain

Vehicle (ATV) as a run around to go with The Beast. Immediately before we met Tomasz, we had passed a quad in the car park and were already deep in conversation about the merits of the cheaper Honda versus the top-of-the-range Can Am.

Our 'King of the Quads' debate dated back to the era B.C. (Before Caravan), when we were definitely buying a motorhome. Although smaller than our new 24.5 tonne pantechnicon, we reasoned a vehicle large enough to live in full-time would be impractical for mundanities such as sightseeing, shopping and, most importantly, getting windsurf boards to beaches down narrow lanes. We arrived at the solution of towing a quad on a trailer as a runaround.

As part of that initial investigation, we had posed the question, "What quad?" to The Shipp Twins. Fastidious researchers and the wellspring of knowledge on all matters camping, caravanning, engineering and general practicality, Andy and Steve did not hesitate,

"Can Am," they expounded in unison.

When you live on a budget, saving a few thousand quid is a big deal. However, in the wilds of Mongolia, the true worth of a resilient working ATV would extend way beyond its value in Pounds Sterling.

"Honda is synonymous with reliability." I opined. "I don't think you can go far wrong with Japanese engineering – and there's no point spending more than we need."

Never in the field of human transport have so many

words been eaten so quickly by so few. The statement had barely left my lips when we ran into Tomasz. When we asked his opinion on quads, unprompted, he confirmed what we should all have learned by now – you get what you pay for.

"We have every make of quad in the resort, but the mechanics in Monte Rosa now only buy Can Am. Our Honda had its engine changed twice in the first year! Are you on WhatsApp? There's a Can Am dealer in Aosta. I'll send you the details."

Tomasz and his family continued up the zigzag but halted their procession of pastel-pink mini-bikes and pushchairs part way up. With four dogs gambolling around their feet, they watched the English couple, who were acting very strangely. They collected water from the stream in a nine-gallon (40 litre) Aquaroll barrel, which they rolled uphill. Then, they emptied its contents into the middle of the deserted hotel car park.

Why?

There was a simple answer. The tadpole puddle was drying up!

Perhaps in Italy, things are different, but to us Brits, finding frog spawn was the zenith of childhood excitement. Mark had already used some old pallets to shade the puddle, to protect its occupants from overheating. On our daily walks, we watched the tadpoles hatch and grow. We had bonded. They were our kin!

As kids, important annual events punctuated each season. Autumn would bring forth blackberries and conkers to collect, while picking bluebells and the miracle of metamorphosis were the main ones in spring. The fascination never diminished; jam jars of jelly collected from local ponds would transform, via wriggling black commas, into perfect, miniature frogs, which we released back into the ponds. After two days of blistering sun, we couldn't bear to see our special, little family of taddys writhing in the mud and asphyxiating as their home-puddle evaporated.

Tomasz had moved on by the time we got around to lifting and moving those muddy handfuls of tadpoles that the replenished puddle waters didn't reach. Then we dammed off the shallow bits with stones to keep more adventurous tadpoles from the danger of stranding.

"Thunderbirds Are Go!" I said to Mark. "We're like International Rescue!"

It was a grimy, soggy, yet worthwhile couple of hours!

Ruby was a fan of the tadpole puddle; she made a beeline for it whenever we took the pups out for their necessaries. She would paddle there indefinitely if we let her. So, it was the first place we searched for her when she went missing.

"*È una nave*" – It's a ship! I explained to Luisa, the housekeeper, indicating the sizeable, square, cardboard box that had been delivered. She looked confused.

"*Un bâteau!*" Mark clarified.

"That's French for boat," I hissed. "I think the Italian might be *'barca'* – where the words 'embark' and 'disembark' come from."

Luisa wandered off looking slightly less perplexed, until she saw us sitting in an inflatable raft on the grass outside the apartment. Clearly, she thought, the English couple have finally lost it.

We'd ordered the boat months ago, in anticipation of exploring water castles in Lithuania – if we ever got there. Deliveries up a mountain in Italy were always hit and miss, but despite an €18 surcharge to compensate for the altitude, the courier couldn't be bothered to locate our apartment.

Luisa was heavily involved in the search for the large and weighty box. A text advised it was abandoned somewhere in the catacombs that formed the underground parking for our two apartment blocks and the hotel. Even if the packaging had not been ripped, we would have inflated the boat anyway, to make sure it was not punctured.

Satisfied that all was in order with the boat, Mark decided to wash Big Blue.

In Italy, Big Blue turned heads. A large, electric-blue van with English plates, adorned with a random assortment of pink, flowery stickers to hold on chunks of peeling paint, it was perhaps the twelve-foot SUPs (stand up paddle boards) on the roof that appeared most incongruous in the Alps.

Encrusted with a full winter's worth of salt, Big Blue was not a pretty sight. The dogs followed Mark to the caravan, now removed to a nearby piece of waste ground in line with the pointless rulings of The Hotel Manager and The Italian Jobsworth. There, Mark retrieved a bucket and rag to do the deed.

I did the only decent thing and established myself on a bean bag with my Kindle and a cup of tea, ready to enjoy the warm sunshine.

A little while later, a sixth sense prompted me to ask, "Where's Ruby?"

"Oh, she'll be around," Mark replied.

"Did she come back from the caravan?"

Mark didn't know.

Ruby does enjoy a mooch and a wander, but never too far. She always checks back regularly to make sure Mum and Dad are still within an acceptable distance. On walks, with one paw raised, her head periodically pops up like a meerkat, and she has the best recall of all The Fab Four. I called her, but she didn't come.

"I haven't seen her for a while. I'll go and look."

I checked all her favourite haunts; the tadpole puddle in the hotel car park; the stream near the Oagre chapel; the stagnant ditch by the caravan – she was nowhere to be seen. I called her again and again to no avail. A knot of fear began to unravel within my stomach. She loves water, so my innate panic overdrive kicked itself straight into top gear. My mind voiced questions such as random worry #27,

What if she's gone down to the River Lys? It's a torrent of freezing-cold meltwater. The rapids would wash her away in a moment!

Of course, when I checked, there was no trace of her there, which was a good thing – or not. Was I already too late?

When the snow bridge collapsed, I had automatically downgraded random worry #32; *a dog swept underneath, trapped and drowned*; and #33; *the bridge collapsing with someone on top of it*, so that was no longer a concern.

I walked around the apartment block, calling for Ruby. Almost fifty per cent of our neighbours, a Milanese couple who had relocated from the city when lockdown eased, were sunbathing on the terrace.

"*Ha visto il cane marrone?*" – Have you seen the brown dog? I asked. They hadn't.

By now, even Mr. You-Worry-Too-Much-Everything-Will-Be-All-Right was becoming less blasé. He abandoned Big Blue's ablutions, and we both orbited the apartment and gardens in opposite directions, calling for her. Because of her beautiful, foxy-red colour, Ruby always attracts the most attention. One of my Top Ten random worries surfaced; *had someone kidnapped her*?

I tried to reassure myself. The village was deserted. There was no one there. I pushed away scary thought #19 relating to the reputedly well-established wolf population in Monte Rosa. A man in St. Jean told us he had seen wolves stalking around a restaurant, right in the centre. And wolves were the reason cited for Pepé, the English Setter, being removed by his owner Stefano from the mountain hut, Der Shopf, in Alagna.

"I'll drive into the village and look for her," Mark said.

As he pulled open Big Blue's door, a familiar fuzzy red face greeted him.

Ruby had climbed unseen into the huge, comfy dog bed behind Big Blue's seats for a quiet snooze and had been closed in. Happy to get a bit of shuteye and unaware of the commotion she had caused, Ruby looked slightly shocked as Mark and I squeezed her tightly between us in a group hug and jointly kissed her all over. I could have cried with relief at getting my beautiful little girl back. Even though strictly, she hadn't actually gone anywhere...

So, between rescuing Ruby, thousands of tadpoles, turning the lawn into a shipping lane, then driving a van with an eclectic paint job and surfboards on the roof around the mountains, we upheld the stereotype of English eccentricity. Not only that, we declared Can Am The King of the Quads.

It was a busy week!

27. WHO STOLE MY MORNING ROUTINE?

Farewell the tranquil life!

In my past life, I loved to begin my working day in bed with a cup of tea and a book. It felt like a stolen moment. Half an hour of 'me' time to collect myself before I had to face the relentless daily scramble of dashing around the country to earn a living, selling high-tech equipment to industry.

Since we gave up work, morning is a favourite time. Having left behind the world of targets, deadlines and stress, it feels so luxurious to wake up naturally and ease ourselves into the day without rushing.

In our deserted Italian ski resort, we would throw open our wooden shutters and sit in bed with a coffee. The apartment was not overlooked, so with utter disdain for the demands of the built-in MDF bedside tables and headboard, which dictated the direction our bed should face, we moved our divan to the wall facing the French doors.

This opened up a magnificent panorama of mountains; an aspect spurned by the architect in favour of a view towards the integrated, faux-pine wardrobe. Also crafted from MDF, it matched the integral abominations on the opposite side of the room. Luckily, the fake wood panelling surrounding the French doors was a continuation of the built-in furniture, so we got the best of both worlds. An arresting mountain panorama, framed by the interior design ecstasy of MDF tongue-and-groove.

As we chatted, read or admired the outlook, warm, sleepy puppies snuggled in for a cuddle. Experts differ on the merits of allowing your fur babies to sleep with you. Some behaviourists say it's bad, because it dents your kudos as pack leader. Some medical professionals say it's good, because it has mental health benefits and boosts your immune system. And some cheeky friends say, "But what about Mummy and Daddy's special moment?"

We say, "Mind your own business!" and maintain that dogs on the bed makes the entire pack happy, while adding a colossal cuteness factor to the pack leaders' lives. (And, as for the other matter, love always finds a way!)

The day unfolds with Lani inverting for a tummy tickle the second she senses one of us is conscious. Stop tickling and you risk an immediate assault from

The Paw – a series of sharp scratches that demand, "GIVE LOVE – OR ELSE!"

Kai is not a morning person. With a confused expression, he shoots bolt upright as soon as anyone stirs, before finally coming to terms with the sensation of wakefulness by settling straight back into slumber. Often, his furry little face will nuzzle deep into your neck, which cannot fail to make your heart melt.

Ruby leaps up to wag her tail and look pleased with herself. She parades stiff-legged across the duvet to initiate her yoga stretches: down dog; up dog; followed by an adorable, suppressed yawn in which her lips curl back just enough to show miniature, pearly-white incisors. Try to get up before she's ready and our demanding little princess will have her paws on your shoulders to push you down, so she can cosy up for a hug.

Occasionally, Rosie might summon sufficient patience to rest between your legs, although mostly, she keeps a vigil from the foot of the bed; glued to the windows to make sure she doesn't miss a thing.

As winter loosened its grip, with enough distance to make it a gentle clarion call, a soft medley of cow bells added to the Alpine ambience.

Once we had come around in our own time, we would take a stroll in clean air, cocooned in our bowl of spectacular peaks. Beyond the Oagre Chapel, we had to wade through a meadow, which led us to the ski lifts with their massive dystopian TV screen outside. Throughout lockdown, it had continued to stream adverts into the blankness of the cosmos. Recently, it had made a spooky transition to its summer video loop, even though there was still nothing but hollow emptiness to appreciate it.

On particularly pleasant mornings, we would cross the piste, now green, and carry on beyond the ski lift. Along the pretty path through the woods that lined the steep valley side, wild flowers had replaced deep snow. Rivulets of meltwater twinkled and chattered through a tumult of rocks, mottled in the sunlight. With or without this woodland extension to our walk, we would return for breakfast through the village centre, accompanied only by the rushing of the River Lys. Our slow starts were the epitome of relaxation, peace, and tranquillity.

It came as a shock, therefore, to be awoken at 7 a.m. by a JCB picking up boulders just outside our bedroom window. It used its perforated bucket to shake them free of soil, then allowed them to crash from a height into the metal bed of a lorry. Since we gave up work, the time of day known as 7 a.m. is dead to us, unless we have a ferry to catch or a vital appointment that we couldn't arrange for late afternoon.

The walls of the hotel and two apartment blocks amplified the restful clang, clatter and accompanying roar of engines. Then, the reverberations echoed back from the craggy, three-thousand-foot face of Telcio, our neighbouring mountain. By then, the commotion had achieved a level sufficient to register as a significant seismic disturbance on the Richter scale.

Finally, it seemed, The Block Management had got around to removing the giant heaps of rubble in the garden. A curious project to add windows into the underground garage had generated the mounds. It was a costly and prolonged program of works (the same piles of rubble were there the previous year), it was also one whose purpose we struggled to comprehend.

Part of the subterranean parking area shared the same picturesque outlook as our apartment, although the rest overlooked the back of the hotel. They had boarded up the new windows, so we were not convinced they had done this for the view. Why would you go to the trouble and expense of digging out a bank to expose the buried concrete walls, into which you cut holes, retro-fit windows, board them up, then re-landscape almost the entire grounds to make good the mess caused by the works? All for the seemingly pointless exercise of bringing the outside in to an underground garage, which already had electric lighting on a motion sensor.

But diggers at dawn was not the only shock to our calm, forenoon routine. Our morning pee poo circuit with the dogs became a bit of an ordeal.

Previously, the only hazard had been the Red Dog and the Terrible Terrier. We always say, "You get the face you deserve," and the Red Dog was no exception. He resembled a small Akita, the colour of a ginger nut biscuit. His creased countenance was not unlike Gordon Ramsay's, and like Gordon, his permanent frown was a clue to his nature. Unfenced and unrestrained, he patrolled the perimeter of his home with his snappy, yappy, dirty-white sidekick. Our path first passed about six feet below their lawn, before rising to the same level. This initially gave the Terrible Two the advantage of the high ground.

The offensive inevitably started with intimidating growling at head height, but thankfully out of reach.

"Jackie, you walk on with the dogs while I block," was DD1 – Doggie Drill No. 1: Bypassing Canine Attack.

It worked well, since, with humans at least, the pair were all mouth and no trousers. We knew this because we sometimes knocked on the door of their residence to collect our order of freshly laid eggs and home-produced Toma cheese. These were supplied by the Adler's Nest mountain hut at Gabiet, in the hills above Staffal.

While you could never rule out an incursion, The Terrible Two tended not to wage war beyond the boundary of their own lawn. However, they treated any pooches who approached too closely to a snarling lunge with teeth bared. Sadly, even experience had not yet taught our lovely Rosie to believe us on this. Ever the optimist, she occasionally sneaked back after a successful DD1, convinced that an international alliance with the Terrible Two was still both possible and desirable.

With the warmer weather, the adder came permanently in play. Most mornings, he would be sunning himself somewhere near his hidey hole in the wall.

This would necessitate Doggie Drill 2: Serpent Avoidance. I held everyone in 'wait' mode, while Mark confirmed the snake's precise location. On the all clear, I waved the pups past and physically prevented curious people like Nosy Rosie from further investigations of that twig-thing-that-smells-so-interesting-and-doesn't-move (most of the time.) We made sure never to leave any prospect of opening negotiations in a canine-viper alliance to Rosie's own diplomatic judgement.

Spring had returned to the mountains, and along with it, livestock. Farmers released the beautiful chestnut-and-white Valdostane cows to graze in a different part of the village each day. Their rich milk forms the foundation of the delicious, local cheeses, such as Toma and Fontina. Sometimes the herd was visible; sometimes the faint tinkle of cow bells gave them away, but not always. So, route-planning for our morning walk began with a bovine guessing game; 'Where might The Toma Team be today?'

The cattle posed two hazards. The first being that Lani loves cows. To her, quadrupeds fall into two categories; 'big dogs' and 'things to chase'. Cows are basically big dogs, so why wouldn't you bound up, introduce yourself, and ask if anyone wants to play? We were fairly sure that Valdostane cows remained fully aware that Lani was not one of the girls. They are horned, and renowned for fighting, albeit mostly among themselves, to sort out the herd pecking order. In more normal times, the bovine-based 'Battle of the Queens' is a springtime spectator sport in Aosta.

More worrying than the large and well-armed cows was the accompanying rabble of half-a-dozen hairy hounds. Selectively bred for their immense size, protective instincts and ability to take on packs of wolves and win, they were all mouth, full trouser, and not to be tangled with under any circumstances. The weather-beaten farmers who sat with the herd always gave us a friendly wave, but used restraining methods to maintain an appropriate social distance between our Cavapoos and their canine colossi.

As the herds and flocks returned to the higher pastures, we suspected the risk of run-ins with shepherd dogs might curtail our Alpine walking career for the season.

The final peril was the bees. All over the valley, including our morning meadow, bee hives had cropped up to convert the psychedelic bounty of crazily coloured flowers into delicious wildflower honey. Rosie did not yet believe us on this one either. I thoroughly admired her vision of world peace and inter-species accord, but I suspected she might come around to our way of thinking one day soon. It would happen the moment we turned our backs and she stuck her nose into a hive to prove to us that underneath it all, like every other living creature on the planet, bees are friendly and love dogs.

This was the face of our new normal. As spring got a grip in the valley and Italy returned to work, our morning routine was disrupted: relaxed ambience was replaced with alarm calls at an ungodly hour from a boulder-rattling JCB, and we were forced to run the gauntlet of a venomous snake; bees; horned, fighting cattle; fearsome guard dogs and The Terrible Two.

I asked Mark, "When can I move back to Lambeth?"

Lambeth is the less-than-salubrious part of central London where I lived when I took up my first 'proper' job as a researcher in St. Thomas' Hospital Medical School. Home was the 19th floor of a tower block, whose soulless windows frowned down upon Battersea Power Station, and the upper surfaces of planes flying up the Thames into Heathrow. It was so high, it sometimes swayed noticeably in the wind. Both lifts smelled of pee – and inevitably broke down on shopping day.

While waiting in the lift lobby on my way home from a job interview, I was robbed. I reported the crime and gave a statement. The police later caught the mugger and called me in to identify him. I had provided an accurate description because stupidly, I had fought against him. He dragged me up two flights of stairs before the handle of my bag broke and he made off through a second-floor exit.

Besides my bag, he had my keys, wallet and address, because it was the one day I was carrying an interview letter, which directed me where to go. What's your luck?

When I asked the police how they managed to apprehend him, the officer told me that the man who had robbed me and had my keys and address was, "...wanted in connection with a murder."

28. CARVINGS, CHAMOIS & A CHANGE OF PERSPECTIVE

"Shoot for the moon, and even if you miss, you'll land among the stars." [1]

This quote is attributed variously to positive thinkers Norman Vincent Peale and Les Brown. It is not true, of course.

I am a scientist and feel obliged to point out that the sun, our nearest star, is four hundred times further from Earth than the moon. But I like the sentiment.

Trapped in a deserted ski resort in Italy, Mark and I had been obliged to re-think our targets – and not just because of coronavirus.

My Dad introduced me to mountaineering. "Once I'm up here, I never want to go down," he once told me, as he contemplated creation from the summit of Snowdon. From Wales' highest peak, I couldn't help but agree. I felt like I was on the roof of the world.

I took my friend's fourteen-year-old son up Starling

Dodd in the UK's Lake District. Alex lived in the Netherlands and had never seen a mountain, never mind climbed one. On the top, he spontaneously set off like Julie Andrews in *The Sound of Music,* leaping and twirling through the heather. He whooped and laughed with excitement. Witnessing such pure, unfettered joy from a moody teenager is among my most treasured memories, but mountains can do that to you. They give you a change of perspective.

And talking of mountains, do you know your Munros, Corbetts and Grahams?

Munros are Scottish mountains with an altitude greater than 3,000 ft (914.4 m) – plus a little social distancing. If the summits are too close together, they are not 'Marilyns', as those in-the-know call 'proper' Munros. They are merely 'Munro Tops'.

'Munro Baggers' are the elite force of mountaineers who aim to climb all 282 of them – or 509 if you include the Tops.

Your Corbetts and Grahams are more minor peaks. The 222 Corbetts rise between 2,500-3,000 ft (762-914.4 m). At a paltry 2,000-2,499 ft (610-761 m), a Graham is one of the 212 Peaks-Formerly-Known-As-Lesser-Corbetts.

Munros are the tallest mountains in the UK. At 4,413 ft (1,345 m) 'The Ben' (Ben Nevis) is the mightiest of them all.

Mark and I have climbed a few Munros. The toughest is Sgùrr Dearg, which is as difficult to conquer as it is to pronounce. The true apex of 'Scure

Jerrack', which means 'Red Peak' in Scottish Gaelic, is the 'In Pin' or 'Inaccessible Pinnacle'. Bagging Dearg requires an airy clamber up a narrow fin of rock using ropes, with dizzying drops on either side.

As conquering heroes, Mark and I lay prone across Dearg's 'non-summit'. With the In Pin soaring above us, we were too terrified to sit up and eat our sandwiches, never mind dangle off its knife edge. So, Dearg is the only mountain ascent we have ever tackled without bagging an actual summit. Until...

Staffal sits beneath another Red Peak – the Rothorn, although this one exists on an entirely different scale. You might think The Ben is big, but it's just peanuts compared to the peaks around Monte Rosa. Rothorn rises to 3,000 metres, not feet – think three-and-a-bit of your basic Munros piled on top of each other. And while the Rothorn is a 3M (Three Munro), it is not even one of the Big Boys. Dufourspitze, Monte Rosa's Top Spot, is the second highest peak in Western Europe. At 4,634 m, Dufour is a Five Munro; a touch above 15,000 ft.

Our functional dog walk up the zigzag path next to our apartment involved an ascent of almost exactly 1,000 ft – or half a Graham. In the Alps, that's just a stroll, and even after all that climbing, it's miles below the peak of the Rothorn. Unless you limit yourself to the valley floor, the hikes in Gressoney are all up. And very steeply up at that!

Kai is shy of other dogs, so we were delighted when he struck up a bit of a bromance with our Italian neighbour, Lampo. Although he was supposed to be taking it easy, Lampo had sneaked out to walk with us for the first time in ages. A few days previously, in floods of tears, his mum, Luisa, explained that he was going to be 'done'. He had spent most of the previous week tied up because a bitch in the village was in season.

Luisa spoke no English. The subject of castration tested our conversational Italian, but we had reassured her that Kai was *castrato;* that the procedure was pain free, involved a quick recovery, and was ultimately beneficial for the dog. Thus, with only one pair of testicles between us, our crew of seven set out to walk to Bedemie, a favourite mountain refuge. We had christened it 'The Cuckoo Hut' because a home-made bellows contraption welcomes you with a cuckoo whistle as you open the door.

I have a long-held disdain for dandelions. As kids, we were told that if we picked them, we'd wet the bed, and if we blew a dandelion clock, we'd never be a gardener's friend. When we lived 'in the brick', I used to squander an inordinate amount of precious leisure time trying to lever this prolific and pestilential weed out of my front lawn with a special tool. It became an obsession. As my hands blistered with the effort, I often mused that if pesky dandelions were a cash crop, I'd be rich.

Just before we started our climb, we met a young woman harvesting dandelion heads from the bright sea of yellow that had washed over the meadows around the village.

"Why?" we asked her.

"I boil them with sugar, lime juice and water to make a syrup," she told us. "It is good for the throat."

Well, knock me downy with a feathery seed head. Dandelions have a purpose!

I thought the syrup sounded quite nice, but until I looked up a recipe later, I had no idea of the multitudinous merits of a dandelion. They are tasty (apparently!), nutritious, have medicinal properties – and bees love 'em.

You can make them into caffeine-free tea, coffee, salad, pesto, wine, soap, shampoo, anti-inflammatory muscle rub, yellow dye and cupcakes. They contain more beta carotene (vitamin A) than carrots and are packed with minerals, anti-oxidants and vitamins.

Medical claims state they are anti-bacterial, strengthen bones and immune function, help regulate cholesterol, aid digestion, prevent cognitive decline, remove warts, protect skin against premature ageing, kill leukaemia cells without affecting healthy cells, and have proven potential in treating other kinds of cancer.[1]

And they are diuretic, so in theory, they could make you wet the bed.

If only I'd known. On my weed-riddled lawn, I was sitting on a goldmine. Literally!

At the edge of the track up to Bedemie, we noticed

some wooden sculptures for the first time. They had been covered by snow when we walked there in another life, with our Dutch friends, Casper and Monique, a few months before. We suspect The Cuckoo Hut's owner created them. A real-life woodcutter, he is the image of a fairy tale character. He has a kind, gentle face, and always sports a bandana over his wispy white hair.

Working with wood is a popular craft in the area, and in the past, making toys and decorations was one way to help pass the long winter evenings. The traditional *stadel* houses, built by the local Walser people, were constructed from wood and stone. Grotesque faces, carved into tree stumps, are also a common sight around the valley.

When we reached Bedemie, our panorama took in Orsia, a pretty hamlet composed mostly of eighteenth-century *stadels*. Close up, many have religious writing or symbols carved into the ridge beams. We could clearly see a fenced *gassò* (a path enclosed by walls or fences to prevent livestock in transit from disturbing crops), which connected Orsia with the hillside pastures of Bedemie.

Along the main road above Orsia, we looked down on Selbsteg, literally 'the bridge that made itself'. There, an enormous boulder wedged between the cliffs of the narrow gorge has created a natural crossing over the River Lys.

Rothorn towered above Selbsteg and Biel, whose very name means 'summit'. There, on a knoll to protect the buildings from floods, the petite white chapel *Cappella di Santo Rocco e Santo Sebastiano* was founded after the plague of 1630. Rather appropriately, these two saints are protectors against epidemics. We quietly thanked them for doing an admirable job, since throughout the coronavirus pandemic in the hotspot that was Northern Italy, there had been zero cases of COVID-19 in the upper Gressoney valley.

It was too gorgeous to turn back, so we hatched an ambitious plan to do a circuit by walking up the red ski run towards the lift station at Gabiet, then returning down the black slope, Moos.

We cut a corner via one of our off-piste routes. In the trees, through which we once skied deep, fluffy Japanese-style powder with our wonderful Scottish guide, Dave, we saw an ibex. It was the more usual view of a *stambecco* – distant and obscured. Not the princely poses afforded to us by the herd that we had by now encountered on every walk above our residence at Courtlys.

Devoid of snow, we realised the red piste was actually a road – and it made a huge scar on the landscape. For many years, the environmental lobby has opposed the proposed lift to connect Monte Rosa with Cervinia and Zermatt. If it went ahead, it would create the third largest ski area in the world. Seeing a ski resort in summer without the snow made it very clear that there is a lot of infrastructure – and it is anything but pretty.

This project gave us mixed feelings. Rather than skiing down the same mountain, we enjoy going places on skis. We can already do that in Monte Rosa's three valleys – or to a much greater degree in the vast ski areas of Les Trois Vallées, the Vanoise, the Grand Massif, Zermatt/Cervinia or the Dolomiti Superski. Uncrowded tranquillity is what makes Monte Rosa unique. The trouble is, that doesn't contribute to the balance sheet.

The climb left us gasping like Darth Vader at the end of his weekly step class. Cloud obscured the bright spring sunshine, while piles of dirty snow and shattered grey rock surrounded us. It made the top of the black piste, Moos, look bleak and forbidding.

The slope itself was still holding on to lots of soft snow, which made our descent tentative. It was slippery, more precipitous than the ascent, and in places, there were hidden hollows beneath the snow. Mark is six-foot-six (2 m) tall. I have said before that the difference between my husband and a tractor is that one has hydraulics, and the other has high bollo...

Mark fell through the snow right up to them at one point.

A dainty black-and-white chamois goat bounded across the piste, directly in front of us. It vanished the instant it entered the boulder field to our left. As with ibex, it never ceases to amaze me that creatures the size of a small horse are invisible in their natural habitat, especially the ones who hang out in herds!

Mark and I trudged back into Staffal. Our hiking satnav advised we had covered a distance of five miles, with 1,826 ft (557 m) of ascent and descent.

That's the best part of a Lesser Corbett and it was

just an afternoon stroll! At no point had we been anywhere near the top of anything.

This is what I mean about revising our objectives. We had to become accustomed to climbing a multitude of Marilyns and Grahams without ever 'bagging' a thing!

Japanese martial artists used to train until they were deemed worthy of their 'Dan' grade, at which point they were awarded a black belt. Sensei Kawaishi Mikonosuke introduced the grading system of coloured belts when he brought judo to Paris in 1935. He felt Europeans needed the encouragement of reward and recognition to motivate their progress.

Lockdown has enforced a re-evaluation upon all of us and our day caused me think. Are dandelions just weeds? Are we too obsessed with conquering, bagging and achieving? Are Tops any less of an accomplishment than Marilyns, and is the walk still worthwhile if it isn't a tick for your list?

We saw carvings, chamois and got a change of perspective.

It was definitely worth it!

29. INTO THIN AIR

The Universe doesn't get mad; it gets even...

"The Valle dei Principi (the Valley of the Princes) or the Loo Valley are both really beautiful," Ezio from the ski shop in Staffal told us.

He pronounced it 'the Low Valley', but, since I get a childish buzz from places with slightly rude names, it was already marked on my map.

Lockdown in Italy was relaxing, and in a few weeks we would even be able to continue our travels, but in the spirit of 'It never rains but it pours', a relentless fortnight of pelting rain put paid to our grandiose hiking plans.

If you remember, one dry day had taken us to the stunning mountain hamlet of Cialvrino. Since my camera battery ran out just before we stumbled upon our dream house, we returned the following afternoon to photograph it, floating in its sea of orchids. From there, we took a different forest path to the top of the ski lift at Weismatten. When we arrived, the darkening sky dictated we exchange our proposed circular hike around the forested lake for a hasty return to base.

Just as we slammed Big Blue's doors, heavy drops of rain exploded around us. Within two minutes, Mark and I were high-fiving our good fortune at missing the rainstorm, which quickly transformed into a full-blown thunderstorm. A wrong turn in Venice followed by a drive down the Grand Canal could not have been wetter.

Of course, such impeccable timing meant we now owed a debt to the Universe.

A few days later, cicadas chirruped in sunlit, flower-filled meadows as we pulled up in Coumarial, a local beauty spot near the Mont Mars nature reserve. We had walked there several times in the snow, but to grant full honours to the wonderful June sunshine, we had packed a picnic of cheese, salami and fresh, home-baked bread.

It was not the day I expected the Universe to collect on its debt. Sitting out a violent thunder- and hail-storm in a dilapidated cow shed, with decidedly vintage manure splattered over the floor, walls, ceiling, and doors, was not how I foresaw spending the after-noon. We didn't dare touch our picnic for fear of contracting *Escherichia coli*.

"If you hear any creaking – run out of the door,"

Mark said, fearing for the structural integrity of our rustic shit shack.

As rain and hail hammered down, accompanied by sheet and bolt lightning, I wondered what we would do. We were at the exact mid-point of the walk, in the middle of nowhere, and hadn't bothered to bring waterproofs. Why would we need them on such a fine day? When the lightning passed to a safe distance, we made a run for it. It tested the wicking ability of our fleeces to the limit. Suffice to say we got very wet and cold.

The hot water system in our apartment was communal, and they charged for water by the litre. It was temperamental at the best of times, but with the block deserted, it took so long for warm water to come through that we only used it to shower. To wash dishes, we thriftily heated a pan on the hob. All other ablutions fell into the category of 'character building'.

But the Universe wasn't done with us yet. The warming, steamy shower that occupied my fantasies for the entire forty-minute drive home didn't materialise. Despite wasting litres of water, the deluge from our *doccia* (shower) refused to warm up, and I had no desire to build my character any further that afternoon by stepping beneath its Siberian stream.

A quick round through Cortlys had become a

regular circuit along Footpaths 1 and 7. One bright morning, it ended in a hike to 9,000 ft.

"Shall we carry on?" we kept saying to each other, because the weather was so gorgeous and the scenery too stunning to turn back. We continued up towards Bettolina on Footpath No. 1.

However, as dark clouds blotted out the sun on the far side of the valley, we decided to make a push for the top. Had the Universe taught us nothing?

As happened so often in Monte Rosa, there was no top – at least not for a good few thousand feet. Our 'top' was just a flatter bit before the next steep rise. Had we not made that last push, we would not have got soaked to the skin in another thunderstorm on the way down. Mark loaned me his baseball cap to help me find my way, because there was so much rain that without shelter from his peaked cap, I couldn't see through my spectacles.

Stuck indoors for weeks on end, we were bored. So bored. We had plenty to keep us occupied, but had lost all passion for doing the same things, over and over. With my controlled self-isolation from Facebook and the village still deserted, we had barely any social contact. It seemed churlish to complain about our lot when people were dying and healthcare workers were, according to Italian newspapers, 'waging war'. But it didn't mean we were immune from the waking nightmare that reappeared relentlessly every morning.

Being trapped in the apartment because of the elements was all too similar to lockdown. Now, though, instead of avoiding contagion, we were glued to the weather like proper Brits; prepared to shoot out with the dogs the absolute second the skies cleared. Then, at the end of June, after a fortnight of torrential rain and just days before we were due to depart, the season suddenly changed. Summer arrived. It was Monte Rosa's last smile; to remind us how much we love her.

We set out to do our final 'big' walk before leaving. Rather than drive to Loo or Principi, we opted for a trek on our doorstep, the Vallone di Salza, to recce an off-piste ski route that was firmly on our bucket list for the following season.

After four hours of steep ascent, panting in the thin air, we reached 8,550 ft, but were still 900 ft short of the top of the col. We were nowhere near the summit of anything – every surrounding peak fell staunchly into the 15,000 ft club.

Surrounded by dazzling Alpine scenery, drenched in colour, we sat alone on a sunlit boulder and reflected upon our life choices. Lockdown had shone a spotlight on how dreams can so easily dissolve into thin air. Who would have thought that the most routine things in life such as hugging a loved one, or going out for a cup of coffee, would become so precious? That taking a vacation, or even going home, could become illegal?

Lockdown had also given us a glimpse into a common problem with retirement. Without the focus, structure and social contacts a job brings, it can leave a huge vacuum in people's lives. Those much-anticipated days of leisure can so easily become a barren wasteland of time to fill.

On days when I couldn't summon the enthusiasm to do things I love, like open a book, watch a film or write, I'd experienced it myself – that relentless fade to grey. My self-image had evaporated and everything that formed my identity had been erased. I was no longer a globetrotting adventurer, an author, an off-piste powder hound or Mrs. Windsurfing. For the first time in my life, I felt like a frumpy fiftysomething.

At least routine and a lack of variety makes time appear to pass quickly. In lockdown, that had been a blessing. I remember how my working weeks used to blur into each other, while a fortnight's holiday stretched out like an eternity of shimmering bliss.

Our lifestyle is all about exchanging that mental imprisonment for liberty. In retirement, far from narrowing our horizons and winding down, passively accepting the inexorable wane into oblivion, we feel we are surging forwards and growing. In more normal times, our everyday is varied, extraordinary and filled with wonder. We are constantly solving problems, learning new skills, and looking forward to a future that still brims with possibilities.

'May you live in interesting times.'

Was the Chinese proverb really a curse or a blessing? Particularly in our lives, things don't always go to plan – but at least it keeps us nimble!

It was time to return to our dream. In a few days, we intended to embark on a very slow road back to the

UK, via France & Spain. We couldn't go home directly, because Britain was still locked down, but we had lost too much time to circumnavigate the Baltics.

Of course, we considered the ethics of travelling in such times. It was a risk, but then again, there are never any safety guarantees. Europe was opening up, and we figured businesses could use the tourist dollars. In addition, a caravan is the perfect socially distanced mode of transport. We would not pose any danger to ourselves or others, because Kismet was a self-contained hotel room and restaurant on wheels, with every facility we could possibly need on board.

Even though we had been in Monte Rosa for eight months, including three months in strict do-not-leave-the-house lockdown, we agreed it had not killed our desire to return the following winter. Not just to take advantage of the 30% discount on our seasonal lift passes, offered in recompense for the months lost to coronavirus; but for things such as the Loo Valley and the Valle dei Principi. Despite the four ski seasons we had spent in Monte Rosa, she invariably tempts us back with the promise of more to see and do.

Besides, to make room for our new boat, we left Big Blue's winter wheels and all our ski gear in the apartment's ski locker and storage garage, because we would definitely be there the following year. Confident the pandemic would be over, once again, we happily took tomorrow for granted...

Both Mark and I were desperate to leave; to see

something different. Yet we also felt a strong need to return.

We wanted to experience Monte Rosa again as we remembered her; a vast mountain wilderness that spells freedom and joy; not a prison in paradise.

PREVIEW

ADVENTURE CARAVANNING WITH DOGS
BOOK 5

To Hel in a Hound Cart
Jacqueline Lambert
For Publication in 2022

PROLOGUE – A BIT OF A SCRAPE

"I think we're f*****. I don't know how I'm going to get us out of this," Mark's verdict was swift.

Since we'd driven into a situation, it seemed incongruous to me that there was no way to drive out, but when I got out of the cab to look, I immediately saw the problem.

A beautiful morning had broken over Staffal, a tiny ski village, high in the Italian Alps. It had been our home for eight months, half of which we had spent in strict coronavirus lockdown. It was late June, four months after our itchy feet got the better of us, and finally, we were leaving.

Clear blue skies above the Monte Rosa massif granted me the photograph I coveted of lupins sprouting amid the greenery on the bank by the caravan. Their pink and purple blooms contrasted beautifully with the wooden Alpine chalets and snow-covered peaks in the background. It was a perfect day to travel. What could possibly go wrong?

Because of lockdown, the ATM in Staffal had been empty for months, so we stopped for cash a couple of villages down the mountain in Gressoney St. Jean. The Thursday market was in full swing, but we decided there was too much of a queue to buy fresh vegetables. How could we have guessed that this decision would cost us so dearly, albeit not in the way you might expect?

5,000 ft (1,500 m) further down, as we descended the switchbacks into Pont St. Martin, three deafening blasts from an air horn declared, 'Get the hell outa my way!' It all happened in a second. Racing far too fast up blind hairpins, the green front of a thundering truck suddenly filled our windscreen.

On a right-hander that needed a wide swing for a 16 ft (5 m) van towing a 23 ft (7 m) caravan, Mark swerved instinctively, and pulled tightly into the kerb. The truck was left-hand-drive. Through open windows, a broad, tanned face flashed past me, contorted with rage and impatience. He was so close, I could have landed a left hook on his chin, had I not been screaming in terror. He roared off around the bend, unconcerned and unaware that his recklessness had left us in rather a pickle.

The right-hand kerb sloped down into a deep

storm drain. As Caravan Kismet's offside wheel dropped into it, her body tilted and wedged fast against the high stone embankment that shored up the hairpin.

Effectively, we had gone down the rabbit hole. When I looked, I saw the caravan's pivot point jammed hard against the wall, right on the apex of the corner. Whether we drove forwards or backwards, we would sustain serious damage. The best-case scenario was to scrape her side all the way along the rough stones; the worst case was that doing so would rip off her windows, side lights and all other protrusions.

We attracted an audience – and caused a healthy, two-way traffic jam. A caravan is quite the obstacle on a blind bend on a narrow mountain road. The family in the house opposite pulled up their garden chairs to savour the spectacle.

"*Un camion. Un camion è venuto...*" – A lorry. A lorry came... I jabbered away to anyone who would listen. I was in shock, trying to direct traffic, and didn't have the language skills to explain that a truck had run us off the road; that we weren't just stupid English tourists who didn't know how to drive in the mountains. At least I hadn't been at the wheel to attract the inevitable; 'bloody women drivers...'

An Italian parked his BMW behind us and joined in to proffer advice,

"Come backwards. Come backwards. You need to come backwards."

"We can't come backwards; we'll tear the side off the caravan!"

"If we could only get the top of the caravan off the wall," I said, with no idea how.

Mark and I have a motto that sees us through the tribulations of life,

"There's always a solution."

Yet, this time, it seemed the travel gods were testing our resolve.

A REQUEST

Can You Spare Me A Sentence?

Thank you for buying my book. I hope you enjoyed it. All authors appreciate feedback – especially the good stuff – and rely on reviews and recommendations.

I aim to entertain and inform, so if this memoir has taught you something, given you a giggle, inspired you, taken you on a pleasing armchair journey – or anything else – please let others know. You don't have to write *War and Peace* – a single sentence on Amazon, Bookbub, and/or Goodreads would be just lovely.

You might think I am sitting in luxury counting my royalties, but you're mistaking me for Bill Bryson, J. K. Rowling or Stephen King. As an independent author, I don't have the marketing might of a huge publishing company behind me. Many authors never break-even; however, to have even a small shout of becoming successful, all authors need and appreciate reviews.

Reviews are the best way to help readers find books they will enjoy and if you leave one, The Fab Four and I will be eternally grateful. And if you don't want to leave a review for me, please do one for my fellow authors, and we will all love you for ever!

Thank you!

Today is Make an Author Happy Day!

I know. What a coincidence!

If you have already written a review and want to spread the love even further, please could you:

- Share your review on social media
- Tell a friend (or 50!) about my book
- Like a positive review, or mark it as 'helpful'
- Add my books to your To Be Read shelf on Goodreads
- Like and share my blog and social media posts
- Ask your local bookshop and library to stock my books
- Do the same for my fellow authors, we need all the help we can get!

Go on. Make my day!

Keep in Touch

If you want to know when I release new books, here are a few ways to connect with me:

- Follow my blog: www. WorldWideWalkies.com
- Follow me on Goodreads: www.goodreads. com/author/show/ 18672478.Jacqueline_Lambert
- Follow me on Amazon: author.to/JLambert
- Like me on Facebook: www. facebook.com/JacquelineLambertAuthor

I am also a member of We Love Memoirs, the friendliest group on Facebook.

WLM connects readers and authors to discuss all kinds of memoirs, including travel and doggie tails like this one. If memoirs, competitions or book giveaways are your thing, pop in and say 'Hi' there too!

ACKNOWLEDGMENTS

I would like to thank the following people;

Peter, Calvin & the Team at The Hoghton Arms, Withnell, Lancashire – for their kindness and hospitality in our hour of need. We rocked up for one night and stayed for, ahem, quite a while. It gave me the breather I needed to care for my dad – and write the first draft of this book!

Debbie Purse – for her wonderful book cover designs.

Caroline Smith – for eagle-eyed editing and proofing, as well as valued friendship!

Sophie Wallace – @SophieWallaceProofreading for support and advice beyond the call of duty, as well as ever perfect and painstaking proofing. Sophie is also the talent behind the delightful *Deerhound Rhodry* children's books. (Deerhound Rhodry is the canine star of the BBC and HBO TV series *Gentleman Jack*.) Find her on your local Amazon store at author.to/Rhodry

The 'B' Team – (Really an 'A' Team of Wonderful Beta Readers:) **Julie Haigh, Sue Raymond, Andy Hewitt, Susan Jackson, Amanda Stinson Hoffman, Alyson Sheldrake,** and **Lisa Rose Wright** for kindly reading my manuscript and offering their valuable feedback. Andy, Alyson and Lisa are successful memoir authors in their own right. Please visit their sites via the links below:

• **Andy Hewitt** wrote *The Furthest Points: Motorcycle Travel Through Spain and Portugal,* available on Amazon worldwide via: mybook.to/FurthestPoints

• **Alyson Sheldrake** has many books and anthologies to her credit, particularly about starting a new life in the Algarve, Portugal. Check out her website: www.alysonsheldrake.com

• **Lisa Rose Wright** penned the acclaimed *Writing Home* series about life in Galicia, Spain. Visit her website on: https://lisarosewright.wixsite.com/author

Vojin Kremic – for creating the wonderful maps to illustrate each section.

To My Readers Around the World – as authors, we bare our souls for your entertainment. Your kind words, reviews and encouragement mean so much.

And of course, Mark, Kai, Rosie, Ruby and Lani for filling every day with unconditional love and helping me rediscover pure joy.

Dog Bless You All!

ABOUT THE AUTHOR

The author in Monte Rosa with The Fab Four — Ruby, Rosie, Kai & Lani

Jacqueline (Jackie) Lambert is a dedicated doggie travel blogger and author.

B.C. (Before Canines) she rafted, rock-climbed and backpacked around six of the seven continents. A passionate windsurfer and skier, she can fly a plane, has been bitten by a lion, and appeared as a fire eater on Japanese TV.

A.D. (After Dog), she quit work in 2016 to hit the road permanently with her husband and four pooches.

Initially, they were Adventure Caravanners, who aimed To Boldly Go Where No Van Has Gone Before.

Now, they're at large in a self-converted six-wheel army lorry called The Beast, with Mongolia in their sights.

Jacqueline has published five books about how she and Mark went from wage slaves to living the dream. *Fur Babies In France, Dog on the Rhine, Dogs 'n' Dracula, It Never Rains But It Paws,* and *Pups on Piste* all fall within one of her favourite genres; light-hearted travel memoirs. Her forthcoming books will chronicle their tour of Poland in a pandemic, and their new life as Trucking Idiots aboard The Beast.

All Jacqueline's books have received multiple five-star reviews and *Dogs 'n' Dracula* was a finalist in the Romania Insider Awards for Best Promotion of Romania Abroad. *Dog on the Rhine* is a frequent best-seller in Amazon's German Travel and Rhine Travel categories, and on release, *Fur Babies in France* shot to the top of Amazon's 'Hot New Releases', which a statistician claimed meant it outsold Bill Bryson, albeit for a very short time!

Book Bio:
Adventure Caravanning with Dogs Series

Year I: Fur Babies in France – *From Wage Slaves to Living the Dream:* inspired by a group of septua- and octogenarian windsurfers, Jackie and Mark accidentally buy a caravan, then get slightly squiffy and decide to go 'full time' in her. Undeterred by the many breakages and a near death experience on Day 1, find out how they cut their caravanning teeth on the back roads of France.

Dog on the Rhine – *From Rat Race to Road Trip:* follows their adventures through Germany, The Czech Republic, Austria, Slovenia, Croatia and Italy. They get involved with pensioners behaving badly, take Caravan Kismet rafting on the River Neckar, and experience a huge Fidose of Reality when they return home...

Dogs 'n' Dracula – *A Road Trip Through Romania:* warned that they would be eaten by bears, kidnapped by gypsies and mauled by wild dogs, if the floods and riots didn't get them first, see how our intrepid couple get on when they join the mile-high club with their caravan on one of the world's most dangerous roads.

It Never Rains Bit It Paws – *A Road Trip Through Politics And A Pandemic:* five years after giving up work to travel full time, Jackie and Mark race against time to leave the UK before Britain exits the EU. If Brexit happens, their four precious pups will be unable to travel. But Brexit isn't their only obstacle. A few months into their trip, the pandemic leaves them trapped in the epicentre of Europe's No.1 coronavirus hotspot...

Forthcoming in 2022

To Hel in a Hound Cart – *Touring Poland in a Pandemic:* unable to return to the UK due to coronavirus restrictions, Jackie and Mark leave Italy after spending months locked down in a deserted ski village. But dodging adverse weather, COVID-19 outbreaks, and the occasional wild boar, will they make it to Hel on Poland's north coast, or is it their plans that go to Hel in a Hound Cart?

Adventure Travel with Dogs Series

Pups on Piste – *A Ski Season in Italy* contains parables from on piste and off, including getting lost, stranded and conducting experiments on the edge of control, along with a back-country ski course in which the instructor's advice is, "Don't miss the turn, or you'll go over a cliff."

Anthologies

Travel Stories Series & Box Set

Itchy Feet: Tales of travel and adventure – curated by Alyson Sheldrake. A collection of stories from around the world, from the Indonesian jungle to a journey out of Africa that will make you want to pack a suitcase! Jackie's contribution, *Rafting The Zambezi – The River of the Gods* takes you on an adrenaline-infused river ride in Zimbabwe that changed her life...

Wish You Were Here: Holiday Memories – curated by Alyson Sheldrake. We all have that one holiday that stands out in our minds, that one break or vacation we will never forget. Whether it is a childhood 'bucket and spade' family holiday, the 'once-in-a-lifetime' dream destination, your first trip abroad or the city where you first fell in love, the memories are still there today. In this collection of feelgood tales, Jackie shares her wonderful wildlife and romantic encounters in *A Galápagos Fantasy*.

The Travel Stories eBook Box Set contains all three books in the Travel Stories series (the two above, plus *Chasing the Dream: A new life abroad*, which follows twenty brave souls who re-located to exotic places around the world – and we're not just talking about France and Spain.) PLUS seventeen (yes, 17!) bonus chapters – that's almost a whole extra book! In her bonus chapter, Jackie's spills the beans on her second honeymoon, Honeymoon II – The Sequel in her chapter called *A Honeymoon Horror Story*...

Robert Fear Anthologies
40 Life Changing Events: 2022 Edition (Memorable, Inspirational and Life Changing Stories) – twenty-five writers share events that have changed their lives. Some are tragic, some full of joy, but they all encapsulate the tenacity, resilience, and self-belief of the human spirit. This fascinating compilation will encourage you to pause and reflect, with tales that offer much needed motivation and inspiration.

Find my books on Amazon at author.to/JLambert

LINKS & REFERENCES

Chapter 1: Our Exit Before Brexit
References accessed online 27/10/20

[1] 'Law to stop no deal Brexit passed by Parliament' – author of law 'very troubled' by suggestions that PM will not comply with it': (06/09/19) Andrew Woodcock: *The Independent* via www.independent.co.uk/news/uk/politics/brexit-no-deal-bill-vote-house-lords-boris-johnson-law-parliament-latest-a9094741.html
[2] 'What Boris Johnson promised about 'oven-ready' Brexit deal before general election': (7/9/20): Ross McGuinness: *Yahoo UK News* via http://uk.news.yahoo.com/boris-johnson-oven-ready-brexit-deal-general-election-111920698.html
[3] 'PM: I'd rather be dead in a ditch than delay Brexit': (5/9/19): *BBC News* via https://www.bbc.co.uk/news/uk-politics-49598118

Chapter 3: Hints on Heating
References accessed online 30/10/20
[1] 'France's Le Perche Is the last Terroir': (25/3/07)
Colette Rossant: *New York Times* via www.nytimes.
com/2007/03/25/travel/tmagazine/03well.perche.t.html

Chapter 5: Wine and Wonder on a Wet Thursday
References accessed online 11/11/20
[1] Isle of Wight Ferry – a pun!
[2] "God keep us from fire, water and Baron de Vitteaux":
Ernest Petit: 'Les sires de Noyers': *Bulletin of the Society of Historical and Natural Sciences of Yonne*: 1874 volume 28: via http://echo.auxerre.free.fr/
dossier_telechargement/
Bulletin_SSHNY/1874_bulletin_sshny.pdf
[3] "Never doubt the courage of the French. They were the ones who discovered that snails are edible." *Quotefancy* featured in Doug Larson quotes https://
quotefancy.com/quote/1548165/Doug-Larson-Never-doubt-the-courage-of-the-French-They-were-the-ones-who-discovered-that
[4] *Appelations d'Origine Contrôlée* is a guarantee of quality and authenticity for agricultural products such as wines and cheeses from certain geographical areas.

Chapter 11: Back in the Old Routine
References accessed online 27/1/22
[1] 'Brexit: £2.1bn extra for no deal planning':
(1/8/19) *BBC News* via www.bbc.co.uk/news/business-49183324

2 'Government 'stockpiling body bags' says doctor who contributed to Yellowhammer': (3/8/19) by Mia Jankowicz: *The New European* via www.theneweuropean.co.uk/brexit-news-government-stockpiling-body-bags-says-yellowhammer-doctor-54732/

3 Ski runs (pistes) are often graded for difficulty by colour. The usual system in Europe is green or blue for beginners, red for intermediates and black for experts.

Chapter 12: Friday the Thirteenth
References accessed online 22/11/21

1 Rachel Johnson: Boris wanted to be 'world king': (5/11/19) by *Skavlan*, interview with Boris Johnson's sister, via www.youtube.com/watch?v=esSnpTUp-qE

2 'Boris Johnson peddled absurd EU myths – and our disgraceful press followed his lead': (1/7/16) by Martin Fletcher: *New Statesman* via www.newstatesman.com/politics/2016/07/boris-johnson-peddled-absurd-eu-myths-and-our-disgraceful-press-followed-his

3 'The lies, falsehoods and misrepresentations of Boris Johnson and his government': by Peter Osborne: website https://boris-johnson-lies.com/

4 'Why are we so surprised that Boris Johnson lied when he's been sacked for lying twice before?': (27/6/16) by Kirsty Major, *Independent* via www.independent.co.uk/voices/why-are-we-so-surprised-that-boris-johnson-lied-when-he-s-been-sacked-for-lying-twice-before-a7105976.html

5 'Top Brexiteer Johnson penned arguments for staying

in the EU – report': (15/10/16) by Estelle Shirbon, *Reuters* via https://www.reuters.com/article/uk-britain-eu-johnson-idUKKBN12F0U3

[6] 'A reminder of all the Brexiteers who appeared in the Paradise Papers as EU tax avoidance legislation looms': (3/9/19) by Jack Peat *The London Economic* via www.thelondoneconomic.com/politics/a-reminder-of-all-the-brexiteers-who-appeared-in-the-paradise-papers-as-eu-tax-avoidance-legislation-looms-158858/

[7] '£350 million EU claim "a clear misuse of official statistics"': (19/8/17) *Full Fact* via https://fullfact.org/europe/350-million-week-boris-johnson-statistics-authority-misuse/

[8] 'Brexit: Did Boris Johnson talk Turkey during referendum campaign?': (18/1/19) by Chris Morris, *BBC News* via https://www.bbc.co.uk/news/uk-politics-46926119

[9] 'Johnson's suspension of parliament unlawful, supreme court rules': (24/9/19) by Ben Quinn and Severin Carrell: *The Guardian* via www.theguardian.com/law/2019/sep/24/boris-johnsons-suspension-of-parliament-unlawful-supreme-court-rules-prorogue

[10] "The Brexit Party rebadged': Boris Johnson expels 21 Conservative moderate MPs, including 2 former chancellors and Winston Churchill's grandson': (4/9/19) by Adam Bienkov: *Business Insider* via https://www.insider.com/boris-johnson-list-21-conservative-rebels-winston-churchill-ken-clarke-2019-9

[11] 'These are the UK's biggest trading partners': (22/11/19) by Sean Fleming: *World Economic Forum*

online article accessed 22nd November 2021 via www. weforum.org/agenda/2019/11/brexit-trade-uk-eu/

[12] 'China, Russia and Iran hold joint naval drills in Gulf of Oman': (27/12/19) by Ben Westcott and Hamdi Alkhshali: *CNN online* article via **https://edition.cnn. com/2019/12/27/asia/china-russia-iran-military-drills-intl-hnk/index.html**

[13] 'Election Result: 52% of votes go to pro-referendum parties despite decisive victory for the Tories': (13/12/19) by Lizzy Buchan: *The Independent* online article via **www.independent.co.uk/news/uk/politics/election-result-boris-johnson-pro-brexit-referendum-voters-conservatives-a9245866.html**

[14] 'Brexit: Operation Yellowhammer no-deal document published': (11/9/19) *BBC News* via **www.bbc.co.uk/news/uk-politics-49670123**

Chapter 16: Living the Dream in Lockdown
References accessed online 21/12/21

[1] 'The murder of Dr. Charles Budd Robinson': *Kew* via www.kew.org/read-and-watch/the-murder-of-dr-charles-budd-robinson

Chapter 19: The Italian Jobsworth
References accessed online 27/12/21

[1] Eagle Flight and Other Myths Eagles Don't Eat Children or Pets: (January 2008) by Riley Woodford: *Alaska Department of Fish and Game*, via www.adfg.alaska.gov/index.cfm?adfg=wildlifenews.view_article&articles_id=343

[2] Gargantua and Pantagruel, François Rabelais: *University of Central Florida Introduction to World Literature Anthology,* via https://pressbooks.online.ucf.edu/lit2110/chapter/gargantua-pantagruel/

Chapter 20: A Lockdown Lesson for the Environment as Earth Day Turns 50
References accessed online 29/12/21

[1] 'Coronavirus lockdown leads to decline in air pollution over Italy': (17/3/20) by Nick Lavars: *New Atlas* via https://newatlas.com/environment/coronavirus-lockdown-air-pollution-italy/

[2] 'Fake animal news abounds on social media as coronavirus upends life': (20/3/20) Natasha Daly: *National Geographic*: via https://www.nationalgeographic.com/animals/article/coronavirus-pandemic-fake-animal-viral-social-media-posts

[3] 'Link between air pollution and coronavirus mortality in Italy could be possible': (6/4/20) by Aarhus University: reported in *Science Daily*: via www.sciencedaily.com/releases/2020/04/200406100824.htm

[4] 'COVID-19 reduces economic activity, which reduces pollution, which saves lives': (8/3/20) by Maximilian Auffhammer et al.: *G-Feed* via www.g-feed.com/2020/03/covid-19-reduces-economic-activity.html

[5] 'E-bike trials' potential to promote sustained changes in car owners' mobility habits': (February 2018) Corinne Moser et al.: *ResearchGate* via www.

researchgate.net/publication/322991216_E-bike_trials'_potential_to_promote_sustained_changes_in_car_owners'_mobility_habits

6 'Global rise in human infectious disease outbreaks': (6/12/14) by Katherine F. Smith et al.: *Journal of the Royal Society* via https://royalsocietypublishing.org/doi/full/10.1098/rsif.2014.0950#d3e1249

Chapter 22: How the Greatest Rock Climber in the Alps was Saved by the Hunter King & a Poacher

References accessed online 31/12/21

1 'Coronavirus: Outcry after Trump suggests injecting disinfectant as treatment': (24/4/20): *BBC News* via www.bbc.co.uk/news/world-us-canada-52407177

Chapter 24: A Wander with Wild Flowers & Wildlife
References accessed online 18/3/22

1 'Can a lack of love be deadly?': (19/5/16) by Inês Varela-Silva: *The Conversation*: via https://theconversation.com/can-a-lack-of-love-be-deadly-58659

2 'What a Lack of Affection Can Do to You': (31/8/13) by Dr. Kory Floyd: *Psychology Today* via www.psychologytoday.com/us/blog/affectionado/201308/what-lack-affection-can-do-you

Chapter 28: Carvings, Chamois & A Change of Perspective

References accessed online 3/1/22

[1] List of articles on dandelion use in the treatment of cancer: *National Centre for Biotechnology Information*: via https://pubmed.ncbi.nlm.nih.gov/?term= dandelion+and+cancer

-

www.ingramcontent.com/pod-product-compliance
Lightning Source LLC
Chambersburg PA
CBHW021711120626
46545CB00004B/1507